Multicultural Education for the 21st Century

EDITOR

Carlos Díaz

Robert McClure
NEA Mastery In Learning Consortium
NEA National Center for Innovation
Series Editor

D0815753

nea PROFESSIONAL LIBRARY
National Education Association
Washington, D.C.

Printing History
  First Printing: July 1992

Note

The opinions expressed in this publication should not be construed as representing the policy or position of the National Education Association. Materials published by the NEA Professional Library are intended to be discussion documents for educators who are concerned with specialized interests of the profession.

Library of Congress Cataloging-in-Publication Data

Multicultural education for the 21st century / editor, Carlos Díaz.
        p.   cm. — (NEA school restructuring series)
     Includes bibliographical references.
     ISBN 0–8106–3012–5
     1. Intercultural education—United States.   I. Díaz, Carlos
  (Carlos F.)   II. Title: Multicultural education for the twenty-first
  century.   III. Series.
  LC1009.3.M83 1992
  370.19'341—dc20   ® GCIU   92–10059
                                                           CIP

AUTHORS' ACKNOWLEDGMENTS

Valerie Ooka Pang, author of Chapter 4, Institutional Change: Developing an Effective Multicultural School Community, wishes to acknowledge the extensive editorial assistance of Margie Kitano. In addition, Cynthia Park and Ron Evans acted as important sounding boards in the development of her chapter.

The title of Sonia Nieto's chapter, We Speak in Many Tongues: Language Diversity and Multicultural Education, is modeled after a response given by Luis Reyes to a *Time* magazine article entitled "A Confusion of Tongues." As reported in *Speaking Out About Bilingual Education: A Report on the Testimony Presented at the Community Speak-Out on Bilingual Education*, Reyes' response was: "We speak in many tongues, yet we are not confused." (Published by the Puerto Rican/Latino Education Roundtable, Hunter College, New York, NY, June 15, 1983). Sonia Nieto would like to thank Jerri Willet for reading an earlier version of her chapter and providing helpful and critical suggestions for improving it.

CONTENTS

FOREWORD

True multiculturalism and true school restructuring have not often been allied. This conceptually large and practical book narrows that chasm.

It's important that this marriage occurs because too many attempts at school improvement are missing significant opportunities to serve our nation's diverse student body and our country's needs, both now and in the future. That future, by all accounts, should attend to the global, not the provincial; to the multilingual, not just to English; to the richness of our world's cultures, not just to Pax Americana.

This book will become a standard reference in schools working with the NEA National Center for Innovation because it provides the guidance they need to enrich their school-improvement agendas. I hope that other schools will also use this important contribution to the literature of school transformation.

—Robert McClure
Series Editor
Director, Mastery In Learning Consortium
NEA National Center for Innovation

INTRODUCTION

In recent years, much has been written about the demographic revolution in American society and its implications for education. Some writers have referred to this population shift as "the browning of America."

Students of color have always been part of the educational scene in this nation, but their rates of success in our schools have been significantly below those of the majority student population. Two or three decades ago, educators committed to reversing dismal success rates among students of color were often viewed as progressive, idealistic, and even unrealistic by some.

The ensuing "demographic imperative" is causing many Americans, within and outside of education, to realize that this nation simply can no longer afford rates of educational failure similar to those we have had in the past. Demographic growth patterns indicate that students of color, as well as female students, should compose a significantly higher proportion of this nation's professional, scientific, and managerial work force in the twenty-first century. However, this prospect is doubtful if the educational success rates of the late twentieth century continue into the twenty-first. Despite the immense natural wealth of the United States, our future lies in nurturing and developing our intellectual capital. Multicultural education offers a promising vehicle for reflecting cultural diversity in curriculum, classroom, and school practices.

Imagine American classrooms where field-sensitive teaching practices are as common as field-independent ones. In these classrooms, cooperative learning would teach students the value of interacting well with others as well as the rewards of individual achievement. Multiple elements of intelligence would be recognized and rewarded, and students with significant elements of social and spatial intelligence would have avenues to display these skills, along with more traditional classroom talents such as inductive and deductive reasoning.

Teachers in these multicultural classrooms of the future would employ a wide array of teaching methods reflective of the variety of learning styles found among their students. Teachers would occasionally review their lesson plans to monitor the learning modalities being addressed as well as the content. Respect and sensitivity for gender, exceptionalities, and culture would permeate general school and classroom practices. These attitudes would serve as a magnet to increase levels of parental interest and participation in school matters.

Curriculum restructuring would precede operational changes in these multicultural classrooms. At a National Council for the Social Studies conference some years ago, Floretta Dukes McKenzie, former superintendent of schools for Washington, DC, remarked, "It is easier to move a graveyard than to change curriculum." Conceding the difficulty of any attempt to restructure the canon of knowledge, it is still imperative that this nation's curriculum be significantly reflective of national and global variations of culture.

Many Americans have realized that the isolationist tendencies in our educational practices have not and will not produce the globally literate citizens this nation needs for the twenty-first century. Therefore, the concept of global literacy has achieved a modicum of legitimacy and political currency. What is lacking, however, is the notion that we cannot create globally literate citizens who are simultaneously illiterate about the cultural variations in their own society. In other words, multicultural literacy is a precursor to global literacy. This message must reach more of our fellow citizens who have the ability to influence the educational process. American students must understand significant national and global variations of culture and achieve a level of academic mastery comparable or superior to their counterparts in other developed nations. To achieve this, educators and policy makers must be willing to "rearrange the furniture of the mind." Many school practices, ranging from tracking to presenting a monocultural curriculum, derive their legitimacy from tradition, but they need to be re-evaluated with regard to their influence on student achievement.

Invariably, some will oppose any change in predictable practices and routines. Nevertheless, bureaucratic procedures, faculty preferences, and community priorities must be re-examined in light of their ultimate *raison d'etre:* their impact on student achievement. If found lacking, these practices should be changed so that American schools can educate the students who will carry this nation into the twenty-first century.

I am indebted to the professionals who took from their limited time to help with this publication. Particular gratitude is extended to the authors of this volume for their patience and courtesy in working with the editor through the various changes any book undergoes from the conception of an idea to the publication of the work. I also wish to thank those individuals who served as prepublication reviewers; their perceptive comments helped strengthen this volume. While these insights were most helpful, the authors and the editor assume total responsibility for the contents of this work.

—Carlos F. Díaz, Editor
Florida Atlantic University, Boca Raton

Chapter 1

THE NEXT MILLENNIUM: A MULTICULTURAL IMPERATIVE FOR EDUCATION

by Carlos F. Díaz

The United States has undergone a series of societal transformations during its period as a nation. The industrial revolution of the nineteenth century brought profound changes, as did the information and technological revolutions of the late twentieth century.

The twenty-first century, however, may bring this nation its most significant transition to date: a demographic revolution. What once was a country considered to be a microcosm of Europe is fast becoming a microcosm of the world.

Already one in four Americans is either an Asian, Hispanic, or African American, and students of color make up approximately one-third of the nation's public school students (Henry 1990). This demographic shift is occurring primarily for two reasons: (1) The birth rate among persons of color in our society is higher than that among whites, and (2) current and future immigrants are more likely to come from Latin American and Asian nations than European ones.

These demographic changes will have (and in fact, already are having) a significant impact on the curriculum, teaching practices, and teacher and student populations of U.S. schools. It is imperative that we examine these areas now, if we are to accommodate the multicultural needs of the school years ahead.

CURRICULUM

Despite demographic changes in the past two decades,

Anglo- and Eurocentric curricula prevail in many of this nation's schools. When multicultural content is taught, it is frequently presented in an *ethnic-additive* manner (Banks 1988). Material that focuses on ethnic groups is concentrated in special courses and offered as electives in the curriculum. Carlos Cortes and others have suggested that this practice tends to "ghettoize" ethnic content within the curriculum.

A true multicultural curriculum integrates cultural content throughout subjects and grade levels, placing new content where it is pedagogically and contextually appropriate. This *infusion* approach involves a review of the entire curriculum and affects all of the school's faculty. Perhaps these far-reaching demands are what make the infusion method less prevalent than the ethnic-additive approach. Also, because the infusion approach reaches a much higher percentage of the student population, there is a greater likelihood that parents or students will raise the question, "Why do we study this nontraditional material?"

Textbooks, too, play a critical role in the development of a basic curriculum and the ability of educators to make curricular changes. Some educators claim they don't currently teach their subjects in a multicultural manner because their textbooks impede such efforts. These educators may have a point. While textbooks have certainly improved in the past two decades, the wait for the optimal textbook could be a long one.

There is also a political dimension to the topic of textbook publication and adoption. For example, textbook publishers know they will not enhance the marketability of a new American history text by including an extensive and fair discussion of the United States' role in the Philippine Insurrection. Yet, that background would be critical to understanding the notion of Philippine sovereignty as well as in analyzing the contemporary relationship between the two countries. But it is the adoption process that is crucial for publishers, particularly in large markets such as California, Texas, and Florida.

The more heavily educators rely on a textbook as a source of information in a course, the more critical its content becomes. Most educators would agree they should not limit their teaching to information in textbooks. However, multiple demands on their time often leave them with few hours left for selecting and incorporating supplemental materials.

Nevertheless, educators across the United States need to understand that multicultural education is not a fleeting topic whose need and purpose will disappear in a year or two. Schools serve as arbiters of knowledge for every society and provide legitimacy for the information and perspectives they purvey. When they fail to inform students about specific cultural groups, they convey a picture of marginality about those groups in society.

If we were to ask this year's class of high school seniors to name some of the Hispanic Americans they've studied during grades one through 12, the results would be largely disappointing, ranging from no answer, to some Spanish-born explorers, to an occasional correct response. Judging from the results of curricular transmission, one might conclude that Hispanics are all recent arrivals or an infinitesimal portion of the population of the United States. This inaccurate perception is conveyed to Hispanic and non-Hispanic students alike, but the ramifications are doubly serious for the former group.

Restructuring the curriculum to reflect multicultural perspectives requires reconceptualizing our canon of knowledge, not simply injecting selected ethnic heroes or events into an otherwise unreconstructed curriculum. Educators who promote an infusion approach to multicultural education should be aware of such efforts at superficial or simplistic infusion.

Comprehensive restructuring will not only make the curriculum more reflective of reality for students, but will also boost student interest as pupils realize that topics can be studied from diverse, contrasting, and often fascinating perspectives.

TEACHING PRACTICES

A study of secondary school students conducted at Michigan State University in East Lansing found that one-third of all students actively resisted the curriculum, and an additional one-third resisted it passively (Sedlack et al. 1986). Clearly, a great deal more needs to be done in our classrooms to heighten the level of enthusiasm and participation among all students. For minority students, this situation is especially imperative because their rates of academic success are generally below the national average.

The types of instructional methods used in the classroom are of paramount importance. A massive observational study by John Goodlad (1984) showed that instruction based on rote questions and answers is still very prevalent in our nation's schools. Most teachers were field-independent students who performed reasonably well in an individualistic and fairly competitive classroom environment. Therefore, it is not surprising that a look at instructional methods in our nation's schools reveals a large preponderance of field-independent teaching techniques.

However, field-sensitive teaching approaches, which capitalize on human associations, correspond much more closely with the learning preferences of many students. This is especially true for minority students. All students prefer to learn in environments that are most consistent with their learning styles. Approaches like cooperative learning show great promise for involving high- and low-achieving students in common learning tasks. In fact, minority students have shown (Slavin 1983; Cohen 1986) far greater academic gains in cooperative-learning situations than in traditional classrooms.

Other approaches that involve significant interaction, such as peer tutoring or older students mentoring younger ones, also provide promising alternatives for instructing students who are deterred by formal and impersonal teaching approaches.

15

When it comes to examining teaching practices, we need to consider instructional time as well as instructional methods. Time-on-task studies have shown that low-achieving students receive considerably less instructional time than their high-achieving counterparts (Frederick 1977). Because larger numbers of African American and Hispanic students are found in lower-track school curricula, these students are denied the same instructional time as pupils in higher-track courses. This is a rather ironic observation, since those students who are least academically independent should receive the greatest instructional time.

Classroom atmosphere is important, too. After all, this is the setting in which teaching and learning occur. Positive classroom morale has a direct effect upon student achievement. A recent study found that when students felt relaxed and positive in a classroom, they performed better. When they were anxious, their academic performance and self-concepts declined (Walberg 1984).

It is clear that the affective domain plays a significant role in effective teaching. Not enough emphasis is placed on the pivotal role of classroom climate in the education of teachers. Research in this area needs to be an integral part of teacher education if we are to be effective in teaching the increasingly heterogeneous student population of the United States.

TEACHERS

Teacher attitudes and expectations play a significant role in classrooms as well. The bulk of research in this area indicates that racial, ethnic, and social stereotypes affect teachers' perceptions of their pupils. The Pygmalion Study (Rosenthal and Jacobson 1968) found that Mexican American students who made high achievement gains were still rated low in curiosity by their teachers.

Other research indicates that teacher ratings of like and dislike for students also paralleled social stereotypes. In other words, teachers possessed negative opinions of both pupils of color and students of lower socioeconomic status. The body of research strongly suggests that pupils who violate teacher expectations are likely to suffer teacher rejection. This is true even if students who are expected to do poorly perform well (Brophy and Good 1974).

A study was done in Texas to test the applicability of the Banks Ethnic Identity Typology to a cross section of teachers. In that typology, the *ethnic identity clarification stage* is the minimum stage of attitudinal development teachers must meet to work effectively in schools. Fewer than one-fifth of the more than 400 teachers sampled were found to have reached the ethnic identity clarification stage. These results were true for minority- as well as majority-group teachers. Four-fifths of the sample were quite probably unprepared or unable to function in heterogeneous classrooms. Yet the entire sample was composed of in-service teachers (Ford 1979).

The consensus of the literature on teacher attitudes toward minority and lower-socioeconomic status (SES) students seems to indicate that these students, although granted access to our nation's public schools, encounter a rather different climate from their peers. This climate is often less attentive and sometimes even hostile to their educational needs. It is interesting that the data on teacher attitudes show this is consistently true on the aggregate, when few teachers would admit to it as individuals.

STUDENTS

Given the manner in which public schools in the United States function, there are a number of student characteristics that correlate with academic success.

Let's start with the fact that two-thirds of secondary students resist the curriculum, either actively or passively. (Sedlack et al. 1986) Clearly, that resistance doesn't begin in high school, but often considerably earlier. Students who show limited

17

progress in their early years of schooling fall farther and farther behind in succeeding years (Stanovick 1986). There are two main factors behind this phenomenon: (1) Such students continue to find the curriculum to be pedantic and unstimulating; and (2) Teaching practices tend to be unvaried and teacher-centered. The combination of these factors causes students to become increasingly passive and unmotivated with each succeeding year of school.

Educators need to understand that students' cognitive styles are different. While field-independent and field-sensitive students are found in all cultural and racial groups, research seems to indicate that Hispanic and African American students are more likely to be field-sensitive learners. Curriculum presented in a more humanistic and relational manner would be better suited for them (Ramirez and Price-Williams 1974).

The relationship between race, ethnic background, and mental ability has been the subject of much controversy and speculation. One revealing study attempted to evaluate the role of social class in determining mental ability. In this study, an examination was conducted of African American children who were adopted by two types of middle-class families: one white and the other African American. The study found those African American children adopted by white families scored significantly better on the W.I.S.C. test. The 13.5 point difference between the two groups of African American children mirrors the gap in W.I.S.C. scores between whites and African Americans in the larger society (Moore 1985).

A study of socialization practices found that fewer analytic and self-dependent skills were being fostered in Hispanic homes in comparison with socialization practices in Anglo-American homes (Bermudez 1986). This finding supports other studies that conclude that Hispanic students are less numerous among field-independent learners.

Another student characteristic that affects academic achievement is locus of control. Students with an internal locus of control feel better able to affect their environment. Conversely, those with an external locus of control are more likely to feel that factors that influence their lives are controlled by outside forces. When this topic has been related to the socioeconomic status of students, it was found that higher-SES students are more likely to have an internal locus of control than lower-SES students. In turn, an internal locus of control has also been found to correlate positively with higher academic achievement in our nation's schools (Leftcourt 1982).

When you summarize the student characteristics that currently correlate with high academic achievement (i.e. field-independent learner, white, middle/upper class, internal locus of control), it becomes evident that these are not the characteristics that abound in the most rapidly growing segments of this nation's public-school students. Without significant changes in the *modus operandi* of schools, the consequences for the twenty-first century will be daunting.

CONCLUSION

American education must make significant adjustments to meet the challenge of the demographic changes of the twenty-first century. The cultural and ethnic differences between our teacher and student populations are diverging. We cannot continue to assume that all current practices are appropriate, especially in light of the school failure rates for students of color that are frequently more than twice those found for mainstream students.

One place to begin this change is in teacher-education programs. Traditionally, prospective teachers learned about the role of culture in education either vicariously or on the job. Many universities have multicultural education components in their teacher-education programs, but these institutions are currently the exception rather than the rule. Ideally, teachers should enter the profession with a sufficient knowledge of the research base in education so they can relate their activities in the classroom to it. Teachers with these abilities would truly "practice" their profession in a manner more analogous to that of other professionals. This research base should include thorough familiarity with how race, ethnic background, socioeconomic status, gender, and exceptionality interact with the learning process.

A strong component of teacher education should be aimed at assessing a candidate's level of multicultural functioning, with specific strategies for developing respectful and caring attitudes toward all students. Currently, even though teacher attitude is a major factor in the learning process, only in extreme cases would biased perspectives cause teacher candidates to fail to complete their certification programs.

Colleges of education also need to help future teachers develop teaching skills that are relational and cooperative as well as factual and analytical. (Equal time and attention should be paid to the former and to the latter.) Prospective teachers need to internalize the notion that the educational product is much more significant than the educational process. If traditional teaching approaches are not yielding satisfactory results, teachers should not be reluctant to restructure their methods.

School systems across this nation that have not already done so should examine their curricula to see whether or not they present content that incorporates multicultural perspectives. When those perspectives are integrated and permeate entire curricula, they also create an interesting side effect: prejudice reduction. That is certainly another worthy objective for our schools.

It has now become common for educators and community leaders to advocate that global literacy should be a product of American education. The economic impact of not having an internationally literate populace in a global economy is self-evident. However, many have not realized that before persons can be literate in the cultural contexts of other nations, they must first be cognizant of the cultural diversity within their own society. In other words, multicultural literacy is a precursor to being globally literate. The economic value of multicultural literacy will, in time, become as obvious as that of global sophistication.

Public school systems in this nation need to provide incentives for veteran teachers to become familiar with the research base in multicultural education, either through workshops or the recertification process. Nearly all teachers in our schools are interested in improving the level of their practice if new information is presented concisely and in relation to classroom activity. Teachers and administrators must be able to analyze their schools' atmosphere, curriculum, and evaluation practices through multicultural perspectives. If these elements are found lacking, changes should be made.

Finally, educators need to redouble efforts aimed toward students who are malcontent with school or who feel hopeless in their efforts to gain an education. Those pupils need to feel that we, their teachers, believe there are no disposable students.

REFERENCES

Banks, J. 1988. *Teaching strategies for ethnic studies*. Boston: Allyn and Bacon.

Bermudez, A. 1986. Examining the effects of home training on problem-solving styles. E.R.I.C., ED 187107.

Brophy, J. and Good, T. 1974. *Teacher-student relationships: Causes and consequences*. New York: Holt, Rinehart and Winston.

Cohen, E. 1986. *Designing group work-strategies for the heterogeneous classroom*. New York: Teachers College Press.

Ford, M. 1979. The development of an instrument for assessing levels of ethnicity in public school teachers. Ed.D. diss., University of Houston.

Frederick, W. 1977. The use of classroom time in high schools above or below the mean reading score. *Urban Education* 11 (4): 459–64.

Goodlad, J. 1984. *A place called school*. New York: McGraw-Hill Book Co.

Henry, W.A. 1990. Beyond the melting pot. *Time* 135 (15): 28.

Leftcourt, H.M. 1982. *Locus of control: Current trends in theory and research*. New Jersey: Lawrence Erlbaum and Associates.

Moore, E.G. 1985. Ethnicity as a variable in child development. In *The social and affective development of black children*, edited by M. G. Spencer, G.K. Brooklins, and W.R. Allen, 101–115. New Jersey: Lawrence Erlbaum Associates.

Ramirez, M. and Price-Williams, D.R. 1974. Cognitive styles of children of three ethnic groups in the United States. *Journal of Cross-Cultural Psychology* 5(2): 212–219.

Rosenthal, R. and Jacobson, L. 1968. *Pygmalion in the classroom: Teacher expectation and pupils' intellectual development.* New York: Holt, Rinehart and Winston.

Sedlack, M.; Wheeler, C.W.; Pullin, D.W.; and Cusick, P.M. 1986. *Selling students short.* New York: Teachers College Press.

Slavin, R.E. 1983. *Cooperative learning.* New York: Longman Publishers.

Stanovick, K. 1986. Matthew effects in reading: Some consequences of individual differences in the acquisition of literacy. *Reading Research Quarterly* 21(4): 360–407.

Walberg, H. 1984. Improving the productivity of America's schools. *Educational Leadership* 41(8): 19–27.

Chapter 2

MULTICULTURAL EDUCATION: NATURE, CHALLENGES, AND OPPORTUNITIES

by James A. Banks

A great deal of confusion exists, among both educators and the general public, about the meaning of multicultural education. Conceptions of multicultural education range from "teaching about people in other lands" to "educating African-American students about their own ancestry—but teaching them little about the Western heritage of the United States."

This confusion over the meaning of multicultural education was epitomized by a question an editor of a national education publication asked me recently. She asked: "What is the difference between multicultural education, ethnocentric education, and global education?" Later during our conversation, I discovered that she had meant "Afrocentric education" rather than "ethnocentric education." But to her, these terms were synonymous.

THE MEANING AND GOALS OF MULTICULTURAL EDUCATION

A major source of confusion over the meaning of multicultural education is the professional literature itself. Christine Sleeter and Carl Grant (1987), in their comprehensive survey of the literature on multicultural education, found that

23

the term was given diverse meanings. The only commonality the various definitions shared was their view that multicultural education is a reform movement designed to improve schooling for students of color.

To advance the field and to reduce the multiple meanings of multicultural education, scholars need to develop a higher level of consensus about what the term means. Such agreement is beginning to form among academics. The consensus centers around a primary goal for multicultural education, which is to increase educational equality for both gender groups, for students from diverse ethnic and cultural groups, and for exceptional students (Banks and Banks 1989; Sleeter and Grant 1988).

A major assumption of this concept is that some groups of students, because their cultural characteristics are more consistent with the school's culture, norms, and expectations, have greater opportunities for academic success than students whose cultures are less consistent with these factors. Lower-class, African American males, for example, tend to have more problems in schools than middle-class Anglo-American males.

Increasing educational equality for students from diverse groups requires significant school restructuring. That means changing some of the basic assumptions, beliefs, and structures within schools, such as tracking and the ways in which educators interpret and use mental-ability tests. It means developing new paradigms about the ways students learn, about human ability, and about the nature of knowledge (Gardner 1983; Gould 1981). And it means hiring teachers who believe that all students can learn, regardless of their social-class or ethnic group, and that knowledge is a social construction that has social, political, and normative assumptions (Berger and Luckman 1966). Implementing this type of education within a school is a continuous process that cannot be completed within a few weeks or over several years. It requires a long-term commitment to school improvement and restructuring.

Another important goal of multicultural education, acknowledged by authorities in the field but neither understood

24

nor appreciated by many teachers, journalists, and the public, is to help all students, including white mainstream students, develop the knowledge, skills, and attitudes they will need to survive and function effectively in a culturally diverse society. By the year 2000, one out of every three people in the United States will be a person of color. Our survival as a strong and democratic nation depends upon our students' ability to function in a culturally diverse society. As Martin Luther King, Jr., said so eloquently: "We will live together as brothers and sisters or die separate and apart as strangers"(King 1987).

This focus of multicultural education is related to an important goal of global education. Global education seeks to help students develop cross-cultural competency in cultures beyond our national boundaries and to acquire the insights needed to recognize that all peoples living on Earth have highly interconnected fates. Citizens who have an understanding and empathy for the cultures within their own society are probably more likely to function effectively in cultures outside of their nation than citizens who do not have this knowledge.

Although multicultural and global education share some important aims, in practice, global education can hinder teaching about ethnic and cultural diversity in the United States. Some teachers are more comfortable teaching about Mexico than about Mexican Americans who live within their own cities and states. Other teachers as well as some textbook publishers do not differentiate between multicultural and global education. Although the goals of the two are complementary, they need to be distinguished, both conceptually and in practice.

MULTICULTURAL EDUCATION IS FOR ALL STUDENTS

We need to think seriously about why multicultural educators have not been more successful in conveying to teachers, journalists, and the general public the idea that multicultural education is concerned not only with students of color but with white mainstream students. It is also not widely recognized that many of the reforms designed to increase the academic achievement of students of color, such as a pedagogy that is sensitive to student learning styles and cooperative-learning techniques, will also help white mainstream students to increase their academic achievement and to develop more positive intergroup attitudes and values (Slavin 1983; Shade 1988).

Multicultural education must be conceptualized as a strategy for all students for several important reasons. American schools are not working well for most students, as the comparison of the academic performance of U.S. students with students from Germany, Korea, and Japan on international achievement tests indicate. Most students of color (with the important exception of some Asian students) and lower-income students are more dependent on the school for academic achievement than are white middle-class students for a variety of complex reasons. However, school restructuring is needed for all students, due to the current ineffectiveness of today's school systems. (The National Commission on Excellence in Education 1983).

Multicultural education should also be conceptualized as a strategy for all students because it will become institutionalized and supported in the nation's schools, colleges, and universities only to the extent that it is perceived as universal and in the broad public interest. An ethnic-specific notion of multicultural education stands little chance of success and implementation in the nation's educational institutions.

CHALLENGES TO THE ANGLOCENTRIC CURRICULUM

Some readers might rightly argue that an ethnic-specific curriculum already exists in the nation's educational institutions and that it is Eurocentric, Western-oriented, and male-dominated. I would agree with this claim, but I believe that the days for the primacy and dominance of the Anglocentric curriculum are limited. An Anglocentric education dictated our past, but will not dominate our future. The Anglocentric curriculum that is institutionalized within our nation's schools, colleges, and universities is being seriously challenged today and will continue to be tested until it is revised to accurately reflect the experiences, voices, and struggles of people of color, women, and other cultural and social groups in American society.

The idea that only an inclusive multicultural education can become institutionalized needs further discussion because an Anglocentric curriculum dominates today's schools and universities. However, its pervasiveness is much less complete and tenacious than it was before the civil-rights and women's-rights movements of the 1960s and 1970s. The historical, social, and economic factors are different today from what they were when Anglo-Americans established control over the nation's major social, economic, and political institutions in the seventeenth and eighteenth centuries. The economic, demographic, and ideological factors that led to the establishment of Anglo-hegemony early in our nation's history are changing even though Anglo-Americans are still politically, economically, and culturally dominant.

Nevertheless, there are signs throughout U.S. society that Anglo-dominance and hegemony is being challenged. Groups such as African Americans and Mexican Americans are increasingly demanding full structural inclusion and a reformulation of the canon used to select content for the school, college, and university curriculum. Many compassionate and informed whites are joining these people of color to support reforms in the nation's social, economic, political, and educational institutions. Therefore, it would be a mistake to perceive today's reform movements as confrontations between people of color and whites.

One of the pervasive myths within our society is that whites are a monolithic group. In fact, the word *white* conceals more than it reveals. Whites are a very diverse group in terms of ethnic and cultural characteristics, political affiliations, and attitudes toward ethnic and cultural diversity. Many whites today, as well as historically, have supported social movements to increase the rights of African Americans and other people of color. Reform-oriented white citizens who are pushing for a more equitable and just society are an important factor that will make it increasingly difficult for the Anglo-Saxon vision to continue to dominate our educational institutions.

Whites today are playing an important role in social-reform movements and in the election of African American politicians. Governor Douglas Wilder in Virginia, Mayor David N. Dinkins in New York, and Mayor Norm Rice in Seattle, Washington, could not have been elected without substantial support from white voters. Many white students on university campuses are forming coalitions with students of color to demand that the university curriculum be reformed to include content about people of color and women. These student movements have experienced major victories, and the list of universities that have implemented ethnic-studies requirements grows longer each day. It includes the University of Minnesota-Twin Cities, the University of California-Berkeley, and the University of Michigan-Ann Arbor.

Demographers project that students of color will make up about 46 percent of the nation's school-age youths (ages 0 to 17) by 2020 (Pallas, Natriello, and McDill 1989). The Anglocentric curriculum needs to be reformed to include the voices and experiences of a range of ethnic and cultural groups. The significant percentage of people of color, including African Americans and Hispanics, who are in positions of leadership in educational institutions will continue to work to get the experiences of their people integrated into the school and university curriculum. These individuals include researchers, professors, administrators, and authors of textbooks. Students of color will continue to form coalitions with reform-oriented white students and demand that the school and university curriculum be reformed to reflect the ethnic and cultural reality of American life. Parents and community groups will continue to seek a school and university curriculum that gives voice to their experiences and struggles. African-American parents and community groups are the major agents pushing for a curriculum that reflects African civilizations and experimental schools for black males (Chmelynski 1990).

Feminists also will continue to challenge the Anglocentric curriculum because they view it as male-oriented, patriarchal, and sexist. And significantly, much of the new research in women's studies deals with the cultures of women of color (Jones 1985).

THE CHALLENGE TO MULTICULTURAL EDUCATION

I have argued that an ethnic-specific version of multicultural education is not likely to become institutionalized within the nation's schools, colleges, and universities, and that the days of Anglo-hegemony in the U.S. curriculum are limited. This is admittedly a long view of our society and future. Currently, multicultural education is facing a strenuous and well-orchestrated challenge from conservative groups and scholars. This fierce, and at times pernicious, challenge will take diverse forms, expressions, and shapes.

I believe that some of the misunderstandings surrounding multicultural education result from attempts by neoconservative scholars to portray it as a movement against Western civilization, as antiwhite, and by implication, anti-American (Ravitch 1990; Sirkin 1990). The popular press frequently calls the movement to infuse an African perspective into the curriculum *Afrocentric,* and it has defined the term to mean an education that excludes whites and Western civilization (Daley 1990).

Afrocentric has different meanings to different people. Because of these diverse interpretations, neoconservative scholars have focused many of their criticisms of multicultural education on this concept. Molefi Kete Asante (1987) defines Afrocentricity as "placing African ideals at the center of any analysis that involves African culture and behavior" (p. 6). In other words, he defines Afrocentricity as looking at African and African American behavior from an African or African American perspective. His definition suggests that Black English, or *Ebonics*, cannot be understood unless it is viewed from the perspective of those who speak it. Afrocentricity, when Asante's definition is used, can describe the addition of an African American perspective to the school and university curriculum. When understood in this way, it is consistent with a multicultural curriculum because both require students to view behavior, concepts, and issues from different ethnic and cultural perspectives.

THE CANON BATTLE: SPECIAL INTERESTS VERSUS THE PUBLIC INTEREST

The push by people of color and by women to get their voices and experiences institutionalized within the curriculum and its canon transformed has evoked a strong reaction from neoconservative scholars. Consequently, a battle among these groups is taking place. The neoconservatives have founded two organizations to resist multicultural education: the Madison Center and the National Association of Scholars. Their position against multicultural education has been expressed strongly in a recent series of editorials and articles in popular and educational publications. (Ravitch 1990a; Ravitch 1990b; Finn 1990; McConnell and Breindel 1990; Leo 1989).

Many of the arguments in these editorials and articles are smoke screens for a conservative political agenda designed to promote dominant-group hegemony and the interests of a small elite. A clever tactic of the neoconservative scholars is to portray their own interests as universal and in the public good, while calling the interests of women and people of color *special interests* that are particularistic (Ravitch 1990b; Finn 1990). When a dominant elite describes its interests as the same as those of the public, it marginalizes the experiences of structurally excluded groups, such as women and people of color.

Special interest implies a particular interest inconsistent with the overarching goals and needs of the nation-state or commonwealth. To be in the public good, interests must extend beyond the needs of a unique or specific group. But it is important to identify who formulates the criteria for determining what is a special interest. Because the dominant group has already shaped the curriculum, institutions, and structures in its images and interests, it views its interests not as special, but as identical with the common good. Special interests, as seen by of those who control the curriculum and other institutions within society, are therefore those that challenge their power, ideologies, and paradigms, particularly if the interest group demands that the canons, assumptions, and values of the institutions be transformed.

However, only a curriculum that reflects the experiences and interests of a wide range of groups in the U.S. and the world is in the national interest and therefore consistent with the public good. Any other kind of curriculum reflects a special interest and is detrimental to the needs of a nation that must survive in a pluralistic and highly interdependent world. Special-interest history and literature, such as history and literature that emphasize the primacy of the West and the history of European American males, undermines the public good because it will not help students acquire the knowledge, skills, and attitudes essential for survival in the twenty-first century.

An important aim of ethnic-studies and women-studies movements is to reform the curriculum so that it will be more truthful, more inclusive, and more reflective of the histories and experiences of the diverse groups and cultures that make up American society. Rather than being special-interest reform movements, these groups contribute to the democratization of the school and university curriculum. They support the public good rather than the strengthening of special interests.

31

We need to rethink concepts such as *special interests*, the *national interest,* and the *public good,* and to identify which groups are using these terms and for what purposes. We must also evaluate the use of these terms in the context of a nation and world that are rapidly changing. Powerless and excluded groups accurately perceive efforts to label their visions and experiences as *special interests* as an attempt to make their voices silent and their faces invisible.

SCHOOL KNOWLEDGE AND MULTICULTURAL LITERACY

Our concept of cultural literacy should be broader than the one presented by E.D. Hirsch in his widely discussed book, *Cultural Literacy.* He depicts knowledge as neutral and static, and his book contains a list of important facts that he believes students should master in order to become culturally literate. Knowledge, however, is dynamic, changing, and constructed within a social context, not neutral and static as Hirsch implies. He recommends transmitting knowledge in a largely uncritical way. But when we help students to learn, we should teach them to recognize that knowledge reflects the social context in which it is created and that it has normative and value assumptions.

I agree with Hirsch that there is a need for all U.S. citizens to have a common core of knowledge. However, the important question is: *Who will participate in the formulation of that knowledge, and whose interests will it serve?* A variety of people must participate in the identification, construction, and formulation of the information that we expect all of our citizens to master. This knowledge should reflect cultural democracy and serve the needs of all of the people. It should contribute to public virtue and the public good, and it cannot serve only the needs of dominant and powerful groups, as much of it currently does. Rather, it should reflect the experiences of all of the nation's citizens and should empower all people to participate effectively in a democratic society.

32

A TRANSFORMED CURRICULUM AND MULTIPLE PERSPECTIVES

Educators use several approaches to integrate cultural content into the school and university curriculum (Banks, 1991; Banks 1988). Among these is the *contributions approach,* in which content about ethnic and cultural groups are limited primarily to holidays and celebrations, such as Martin Luther King, Jr.'s Birthday and Women's History Week. This approach is used often in the primary and elementary grades.

Another frequently used approach to integrate cultural content into the curriculum is the *additive approach.* In this method, cultural content, concepts, and themes are added to the curriculum without changing its basic structure, purposes, and characteristics. The additive approach is often accomplished by inserting a multicultural unit or course into an otherwise unchanged curriculum.

Neither the contributions nor the additive approach challenges the basic structure or canon of the curriculum. Cultural celebrations, activities, and content are inserted into the curriculum within its existing framework and assumptions. When these approaches are used, the selection of people, events, and interpretations related to ethnic groups and women often reflect the norms and values of the dominant culture rather than those of cultural communities. Consequently, most of the additions reflect the values and roles of the dominant culture. Men and women who challenged the *status quo* and established institutions are less likely to be selected for inclusion into the curriculum. Thus, Sacajawea, who helped whites to conquer Indian lands, is more likely to be chosen for inclusion than Geronimo, who resisted the takeover of Indian lands by whites.

The *transformation approach* differs fundamentally from the contributions and additive approaches. It changes the canon, paradigms, and basic assumptions of the curriculum and enables students to view concepts, issues, themes, and problems from different perspectives. Important goals of this approach include helping students to understand concepts, events, and people from diverse ethnic and cultural perspectives and to understand knowledge as a social construction. In this approach, students are able to read and listen to the voices of the victors and the vanquished. They also analyze the teacher's perspective on events and situations and are given the opportunity to formulate and justify their own versions of them. A key aim of the transformation approach is to teach students to think critically and to develop the skills to formulate, document, and justify their conclusions and generalizations.

When using the transformation approach to teach a unit such as "The Westward Movement," the teacher would assign appropriate readings and then ask the students such questions as: What do you think "The Westward Movement" means? Who was moving West, the whites or the Indians? What region in the United States was referred to as the West? Why? The point of these questions is to help students to understand that "The Westward Movement" is a Eurocentric term because the Lakota Sioux were already living in the West and consequently were not moving. This phrase is used to refer to the movement of the European Americans who were headed in the direction of the Pacific Ocean. Furthermore, the Sioux did not consider their homeland the West, but the center of the universe.

The teacher could also ask the student to describe the Westward Movement from the point of view of the Sioux. The students might use such titles as "The End," "The Age of Doom," or "The Coming of the People Who Took Our Land." The teacher could also ask the students to give the unit a name that is more neutral than "The Westward Movement." They might name the unit, "The Meeting of Two Cultures."

The *decision-making and social-action* approach extends the transformative curriculum by enabling students to pursue projects and activities that allow them to take personal, social, and civic actions related to the concepts, problems, and issues they have studied. For example, after studying different perspectives on "The Westward Movement," the students might

34

decide that they want to learn more about contemporary American Indians and to take actions that will enable the school to depict and perpetuate more accurate and positive views of America's first inhabitants. The students might decide to view a popular film such as *Dances With Wolves* and to discuss the extent to which it gives an accurate depiction of American Indian-white relationships. They might also compile a list of books written by American Indians for the school librarian to order and present a pageant for the school's morning exercise entitled: "The Westward Movement: A View From the Other Side."

CONCLUSION

Multicultural education is necessary to help all of the nation's future citizens acquire the knowledge, attitudes, and skills needed to survive in the twenty-first century. Nothing less than the nation's survival is at stake. The rapid growth in the nation's population of people of color, the escalating importance of nonwhite nations such as China and Japan, and the widening gap between the rich and the poor make it essential for our future citizens to have multicultural literacy and cross-cultural skills. In the twenty-first century, a nation whose citizens cannot negotiate on the world's multicultural global stage will be tremendously disadvantaged, and its very survival will be imperiled.

REFERENCES

Asante, M.K. 1987. *The Afrocentric idea.* Philadelphia: Temple University Press.

Banks, J.A. 1988. Approaches to multicultural curriculum reform. *Multicultural Leader* 1 (2): 1–3

Banks, J.A. 1991. *Teaching strategies for ethnic studies.* 5th ed. Boston: Allyn and Bacon.

Banks, J.A. and Banks, C.A. 1989. *Multicultural education: Issues and perspectives.* Boston: Allyn and Bacon.

Berger, P.L. and Luckman, T. 1966. *The social construction of reality: A treatise in the sociology of knowledge.* New York: Doubleday.

Chmelynski, C. 1990. Controversy attends schools with all-black, all-male classes. *The Executive Educator* 12 (10): 16–18.

Daley, S. 1990. Inspirational history draws academic fire. *The New York Times*, 10 October.

Finn, C.E. 1990. Why can't colleges convey our diverse culture's unifying theme? *The Chronicle of Higher Education*, 13 June 40.

Gardner, H. 1983. *Frames of mind: The theory of multiple intelligences.* New York: Basic Books.

Gould, S.J. 1981. *The mismeasure of man.* New York: W.W. Norton and Co.

Hirsch, E.D. 1987. *Cultural literacy: What every American needs to know.* Boston: Houghton-Mifflin and Co.

Jones, J. 1985. *Labor of love, labor of sorrow: Black women, work, and the family from slavery to the present.* New York: Basic Books.

King, Martin Luther, Jr.; selected by Coretta Scott King. 1987. *The words of MartinLuther King, Jr.*. New York: Newmarket Press.

Leo, J. 1989. Teaching history the way it happened. *U.S. News and World Report*, 27 November 73.

McConnell, S. and Breindel, E. 1990. Head to come. *The New Republic*, 8 January 1990, 19–21.

The National Commission on Excellence in Education. 1983. *A nation at risk: The imperative for educational reform.* Washington, DC: United States Department of Education.

Pallas, A.M.; Natriello, G.; and McDill, E.L. 1989. The changing nature of the disadvantaged population: current dimensions and future trends. *Educational Researcher* 18 (5): 16–22, ff. 46–48.

Ravitch, D. 1990a. Diversity and democracy: Multicultural education in America. *American Educator*, Spring 16–20.

Ravitch, D. 1990b. Multiculturalism yes, particularism no. *The Chronicle of Higher Education*, 24 October.

Shade, B.J. Robinson, ed. 1989. *Culture, style, and the educative process.* Springfield, Il.: Charles C. Thomas Publishers.

Sirkin, G. 1990. The multiculturalists strike again. *The Wall Street Journal*, 18 January 1990.

Slavin, R. 1983. *Cooperative learning.* New York: Longman Publishers.

Sleeter, C.E. and Grant, C.A. 1987. An analysis of multicultural education in the United States. *Harvard Educational Review* 57 (4): 421–44.

Sleeter, C.E. and Grant, C.A. 1988. *Making choices for multicultural education: Five approaches to race, class, and gender.* Columbus, Oh.: Merrill Publishing Co.

Chapter 3

EFFECTIVE TEACHING PRACTICES FOR MULTICULTURAL CLASSROOMS

by Geneva Gay

When teachers are challenged to be more sensitive to cultural pluralism in their teaching, they frequently respond with: "Tell us what to do, and we will do it." Undoubtedly, the demand for multicultural awareness, and the needs of teachers who are trying to meet these demands, will continue—even accelerate—as the magnitude of cultural differences between students and teachers increase, as traditional instructional efforts become less effective, and as teachers experience increasing frustrations and doubts about teaching culturally different populations. While it is tempting to respond to this situation with lists of classroom practices and strategies, yielding too quickly to this temptation is problematic. It may transmit misconceptions and feed fallacious assumptions that effective multicultural education can be implemented easily and expeditiously with little professional preparation.

In fact, achieving teaching effectiveness in multicultural classrooms is far more complicated and demanding than that. It involves three major types of tasks. One has to do with the process of making decisions; another involves assessing the adequacy of the decisions made; and the third deals with how to place multicultural interventions into the proper scope, sequence, and context of other classroom operations.

It is not enough to merely compile catalogs of learning activities, resources, and materials about a variety of ethnic and cultural groups' heritages, histories, experiences, and perspectives. However good these aids are, they are never good enough for most teachers and classroom situations. They tend to be overly general, reflective of their creators' personal preferences and idiosyncracies, and quickly outdated, making their use limited to specific classrooms. Furthermore, catalog listings *per se* of multicultural strategies and activities do not adequately inform potential users about how the ideas and techniques evolved or how to improve the quality of their own pedagogical decision-making skills. They attempt to answer the question of *which* multicultural practices are best without explaining *how* the answers were derived. Rather than teaching teachers how to make quality multicultural education decisions for themselves and the particulars of their own circumstances, catalog listings of strategies may inadvertently perpetuate a sense of personal powerlessness, disownership, and intimidation among classroom teachers.

CONCEPTUAL ORIENTATION

To break this cycle of dependency, and to achieve greater instructional success in multicultural classrooms, teachers need to learn how to make decisions about what is best for their given place, time, and circumstances with respect to cultural diversity. This chapter attempts to respond to this need. It endorses the principle of *multicultural infusion* and proposes that it can be successfully implemented by empowering teachers with multi-cultural education decision-making skills.

Two additional guidelines underline the ideas discussed and proposals made in this chapter. First, instructional decision-making should honor the key definitions, concepts, goals, and beliefs of multicultural education. This requires some fundamental knowledge and understanding of its basic content, conventions, and convictions. For example, advocates generally agree that while multicultural, global, and international education are similar and complementary in spirit and principle, they are not identical. Thus, teaching about Japan, Africa, or Mexico is not the same as teaching about the Japanese American, African American, or Mexican American experience. Multicultural education is concerned primarily with ethnically and culturally different issues within a national context. Fundamentally, it is an affective endeavor, with social reform in schools and society as its ultimate outcome. Therefore, simply teaching factual information about different ethnic and cultural groups' histories, contributions, and experiences, or merely adding multicultural materials to existing school and classroom structures, is not enough. Rather, effective multicultural education requires that values analysis, institutional and attitudinal reform, and social action accompany the acquisition of factual knowledge.

Second, multicultural education should not enter into classroom instruction capriciously, haphazardly, or incidentally. Some carefully conceived and well-planned schemata should be used to govern its *deliberate* and *systematic* inclusion. Several possible schemes are available from scholarly literature. (Banks 1989; Sleeter and Grant 1988; Bennett 1990). However, these frameworks apply more to program planning and curriculum development than to classroom instruction. They are more *conceptual* than *functional* or *operational.* That is, they suggest what should be done and why, but do not explain, with sufficient procedural clarity, how to translate the prescriptions into actual behaviors within the context of real classroom interactions.

Experts contend that because all students need to develop attitudes and skills for living in a culturally, racially, socially, and ethnically pluralistic society and world, multicultural education should be integrated into the learning experiences of all students, in all subjects, at every grade level. But teachers need to know more than this if they are to act upon these suggestions. They must know how to connect these theoretical proposals to the functional operations of their classroom practices. Because learning experiences are dynamic and constantly changing, responding to the "how-to" needs of multicultural teaching with only *product* answers (examples of "what to do") is insufficient. A more effective approach is for teachers to learn how high-quality multicultural teaching practices are developed and how this process can be implemented in their own classrooms. This approach might be called *contextual decision-making*.

Any problem-solving or decision-making process begins with acknowledging and identifying specific problems or situations that require a change in current behavior. After establishing awareness, the problem situation needs to be carefully analyzed to determine its nature and elements, alternative solutions or decisions, and ways to evaluate appropriate options for the given circumstances. Therefore, before quality decisions can be made about what teaching practices are best suited for multicultural classrooms, those aspects of teaching that are most problematic must be identified. This can be accomplished by (1) using *systems thinking* to analyze the structural and procedural elements of routine teaching tasks and functions; (2) identifying the conflict points between these regular functions and their operations in multicultural classrooms; and (3) making decisions and choices about the kinds of changes necessary to resolve these conflicts.

DETERMINING NEEDS

Systems thinking and structural analysis consist of identifying observable uniformities or patterns, functions, and interactions between structures and functions that exist in a phenomenon being studied (Levy 1968). When applied to teaching, these analyses are somewhat analogous to constructing an anatomy of the process. The act of teaching is dissected to discern and describe the characteristics of the structures, tasks, and activities teachers employ habitually in the day-to-day operations of instructional functions. It is similar to, but more inclusive than, techniques that have been used in classroom interaction analysis research. John Goodlad (1984) and his associates used systems thinking and structural and functional analyses in their study of schooling. They conducted site observations in the order to describe the interactive processes evident in actual classrooms, and to deduce from them "who . . .

41

was doing what . . . to whom . . . how . . . and in what context" (p. 226).

Systems thinking about and structural analysis of teaching are based on several assumptions. These are: (1) the process or act of teaching includes some common tasks and functions that prevail across time, place, setting, circumstance, and individual teacher-characteristics; (2) these functions are systematic, habitual, and occur with a high degree of regularity; (3) they have substantive, organizational, and procedural traits; and (4) most, if not all, regular teaching functions have direct implications for multicultural education reform.

These assumptions are supported by the thinking and research of other educators as well. Steven Bossert (1979) suggests that every classroom activity can be described according to its structural and functional characteristics. Goodlad (1984) found some strikingly similar patterns of teaching functions and behaviors across teachers, grade levels, and subjects. Raymond Adams (1970) contends that the classroom is a social and behavioral setting with its own rituals, rules, regularities, and persistent patterns of behavior.

These claims can be extended to yet another level of operations. Not only is teaching a system, but there are other systems (or subsystems) within it, each of which has its own system. Classroom management, feedback provisions, performance appraisal, curriculum design, and classroom discourse are persistent components of teaching. None of these is monolithic or unidimensional. Instead, each has its own elements, structures, and regularities. For example, classroom discourse includes, among other things, who talks when and how, vocabulary, questioning strategies, use of time and space, relationship between speaker and listener, wait-time for responses, and turn-taking rules. Feedback encompasses frequency, quality, praise, encouragement, criticism, prompts and cues, extending student responses, and how these are distributed among students.

Analyses of these various levels of systems in teaching can identify patterns of activities, tasks, relationships, and interactions that comprise the mainstay of classroom instruction and can determine how different students experience the learning environment. Once identified, those in need of change can be more effectively remediated. As Bryce Hudgins (1971) suggests, "teachers must understand how classrooms function if they are to operate effectively and comfortably in them .... such understanding is a prerequisite to the design and implementation of reasoned and viable educational change" (p. 71).

Several different classification schemes are available for viewing teaching systematically and analytically. Individually and collectively, they describe teaching as including methodological, organizational, and managerial tasks; having *preactive* (preparatory) and *interactive* (face-to-face encounters) components; involving *logical* (thinking and reasoning), *strategic* (planning, organizing, and directing), and *institutional* (keeping records, chaperoning, etc.) acts; and unfolding through a progressional sequence of review, presentation-guided learning practice, corrective feedback, supervision of independent practice, performance assessment, and reteaching (Haysom 1985; Hudgins 1971; Jackson 1968; Rosenshine and Stevens 1986).

A composite profile of teaching functions emerges from further explanations of these general characteristics. All teachers, in some form or another:

- Develop and administer instructional plans;
- Set goals and objectives;
- Select content and skills to be taught;
- Create climates and environments for learning;
- Establish relationships with students;
- Teach social and academic skills;
- Choose instructional materials, teaching techniques, and learning activities;
- Appraise pupil performance;
- Provide feedback in the form of praise, encouragement, and criticism;
- Group students for instruction;

43

- Arrange time and space for learning;
- Model and transmit values, beliefs, and norms about social decorum, knowledge acquisition, and codes of acceptable behavior;
- Develop and transmit expectations for and standards of performance;
- Discipline and manage student behavior.

Within and across each of these general functions some specific structures and behaviors predominate. Among these are the passive role of students, whole-group instruction, teacher control, and teacher talk. An emotional tone prevails in most classrooms that might best be described as "flat" in that it is neither harsh and punitive, warm and joyful, passionate and compassionate, nor exhilarating and engaging (Goodlad 1984). According to Goodlad (1984) regardless of what approaches are used to describe and understand what routinely goes on in the classroom, the teacher emerges as the coach, quarterback, referee, and even the rule-maker. But there is no team because "little or nothing about classroom life as it is conducted . . . suggests the existence of or need for norms of group cohesion and cooperation for achievement of a shared purpose." He adds further that "the most successful classrooms may be those in which teachers succeed in creating commonly shared goals and individuals cooperate in ensuring each person's success in achieving them. The ultimate criterion becomes group accomplishment of individual progress. But this would be countervailing to prevailing practice" (p. 108). In the remainder of this chapter, several examples are used to demonstrate how systems thinking about teaching functions operates, and the types of instructional possibilities it can generate for multicultural classrooms.

EFFECTIVE TEACHING PRACTICES

This section takes four major teaching functions and

shows how to use systems thinking and structural analysis to develop instructional change strategies for each. The four functions are: managing instruction through teacher talk, providing students with conceptual examples, transforming curriculum, and creating classroom climates for learning. All four functions play a significant role in the overall instructional process. They also are consistent with the underlying message of infusion as the best way to determine the placement and alignment of multiculturalism in the total educational enterprise. In other words, they support the belief that multicultural education initiatives should impact the significant, mainstream, and regular operations of the classroom, instead of be relegated to the insignificant and peripheral aspects, or be reserved for special occasions.

Teacher Talk

When it comes to classroom discourse, teachers dominate the verbal scene and control the verbal opportunities and tasks of students. They do this through their own verbal initiations and determinations of who else will talk, when, and under what circumstances (Cazden 1986). Hudgins (1971) declares that "someone is talking in classrooms about two-thirds of the time, and about two-thirds of that time it is the teacher" (p. 71). Teachers spend great amounts of time informing, telling, explaining, demonstrating, questioning, illustrating, directing, controlling, monitoring, evaluating, and modeling. Obviously, then, teacher talk should be high among the priority areas targeted for change in developing effective teaching strategies for multicultural classrooms.

Thomas Hurt, Michael Scott, and James McCroskey (1978) argue that effective communication is the single most important prerequisite to successful teaching and learning. Sociolinguistic research provides several different structural, substantive, and procedural components of classroom communication between students and teachers that affect the kinds of

45

opportunities culturally different students receive to participate in the instructional process. They are turn-taking rules, attending and attention-giving behaviors, wait-time for responses, length of speech exchanges, questioning strategies, and feedback mechanisms. Teachers assume that only they have the power and authority to grant permission for students to engage in classroom discourse, and that a single set of rules governing the participation apply identically to all students in virtually every situation. Among these rules are: (1) serialized turn-taking with "only one speaker at a time"; (2) students raising hands and waiting to be recognized by the teacher before talking; (3) maintaining eye contact with the teacher as a sign of paying attention; (4) posing questions to specifically targeted individuals instead of to the group as a whole; and (5) creating a dichotomous relationship between speaking and listening in which the listener assumes a passive, receptive posture. Teachers also tend to use rather lengthy speech segments in giving information and instructions, but they provide small amounts of wait-time for students to formulate and present responses. Questions that require higher-order thinking skills, physical action, and genuine affective reactions are used infrequently, and rarely is anything more than perfunctory praise and encouragement given to students on their contributions.

Some culturally different students find these rules of behavior prohibitive to their classroom participation because they are not compatible with their own cultural rules of communication. For example, eye aversion is practiced among all major groups of color in the United States as deference to authority. Many students from these groups will not look directly at teachers when they are talking. Yet they can be listening intently. Asian Americans, Native Americans, and children whose first language is not English may require more wait-time to provide responses than teachers routinely give because of their cultural socialization and the processes involved in foreign language production. African American and Hispanic speakers are very dramatic, emotional, and active in their responding behaviors. These preferences may result from the prominence of story telling and affective expressions in their traditional cultures. Many youngsters want to establish personal relationships with teachers and depend upon the overt encouragement and praise of teachers to stimulate their efforts. Therefore, the "what" and "how" of teacher talk in the classroom need to be changed to reflect sensitivity to the cultural backgrounds of different students. These modifications might include:

- Extending wait-time and changing turn-taking rules to honor the timing and pacing of different ethnic and cultural groups' participation styles;
- Using alternative cues to indicate attending behaviors, such as asking students to summarize points previously made, to restate another's point of view, or to declare their personal preferences on issues under discussion;
- Shortening the length of teacher speech exchanges;
- Minimizing teacher talk through the use of more student-focused and active learning strategies, such as small-group tasks, simulations, role playing, dramatic readings, and cooperative learning;
- Providing opportunities for students to establish, monitor, manage, and correct their own rules of classroom discourse;
- Allowing the naturalistic discourse patterns of different cultural groups to operate for some instructional experiences. For example, teachers might encourage students to use cultural styles of story telling to develop and appraise translation and comprehension skills in reading, to present critical incidents in social studies, or to report the results of inquiry exercises or research topics;
- Asking more divergent, high-order cognitive and affective questions that allow all students the chance to respond, and accepting their affective reactions as

legitimate contributions to the learning process.

Cognitive Content of Instructional Behaviors

A careful look at how time is allotted across the content of instructional talk is as revealing as its structural characteristics. Much of the actual act of teaching is devoted to providing examples, illustrations, vignettes, scenarios, and anecdotes to demonstrate the meanings and functions of the concepts, ideas, facts, principles, and skills being taught. The process begins with naming, defining, and explaining the phenomenon being taught. All other subsequent instructional efforts are devoted to illustrating how, when, and where it operates. The examples and illustrations act as "pedagogical bridges" between what is being taught in its abstract form and its connection to the life experiences of learners. As such they are the conduits or transmitters of meaningfulness in learning. Thus, the theory of probability, a literary analogy, a moral dilemma, or the concept of interdependence become meaningful to different students to the extent that the examples used to illustrate them reflect the experiences, perspectives, and frames of references of a variety of cultural, ethnic, and social groups. When teachers fail to use culturally relevant teaching examples and illustrations, they minimize their own instructional effectiveness as well as make learning more problematic for students. Presumed "practical" examples of abstract content, concepts, principles, and skills push learning mastery even further beyond the grasp of culturally different students.

An important way to counteract negative responses and make teaching and learning more effective in multicultural classrooms is to broaden the pools of teaching examples so that they are culturally pluralistic. This requires that teachers understand the function of examples in their teaching behaviors, the types of examples they currently use, and the cultural limitations they contain. They then need to determine what kinds of examples are best suited for different cultural groups; how to create, locate, and solicit them; and how to incorporate them into regular teaching repertoires and routines. None of these essential decisions can be made without a working knowledge of different groups' cultural traditions, value systems, learning styles, communications patterns, world views, and styles of interpersonal interactions.

Multicultural teaching examples serve many functions simultaneously. In addition to functioning as "bridges of meaningfulness" between academic abstractions and practical living, they help all students learn about cultural pluralism as they develop their academic skills; they demonstrate that cultural pluralism is a real, normative, and valued fact of daily life in the classroom; and they model how multiculturalism should (and can) penetrate the inner core of the teaching and learning processes. For example, showing how basic mathematical forms or shapes like lines, circles, squares, and triangles are applied in different types of ethnic achitecture (such as Native American long houses, Moslem mosques, Jewish synagogues, indigenous African homes, and American schools), arts, and symbols make them easier to learn for some students. Using ethnic examples of protest poetry in the process of teaching literary-criticism skills may cause some students to be more interested in and improve their mastery of the task. It also introduces all students to multicultural content within the context of studying a normal literature theme and/or genre; and it teaches several different kinds of skill development—literary criticism, critical thinking, ethnic and cultural literary, infusion of multiculturalism— simultaneously.

These illustrations demonstrate the significance of examples in teaching and the powerful potential they offer for making instruction more effective for a greater variety of students in multicultural classrooms. They work well because they validate and employ culturally different frames of reference as aides to instructional efforts while teaching students about cultural diversity in standard disciplinary frameworks.

Multicultural Curriculum Development

A third area of regular teaching behaviors that can facilitate better instruction in multicultural classrooms is curriculum development. Teachers are always designing and modifying plans for instruction. They should understand this function systematically and know how to incorporate multicultural content and perspectives within it. That is, they should be able to transform the curriculum to make it more culturally pluralistic.

Typically, curriculum as a plan for instruction includes six components—rationale, goals, objectives, content, activities, and evaluation. Materials, resources, and time lines are often included as well. These components can be further grouped by function and value into two categories. One is substantive and intrinsic; the other is methodological and instrumental. The substantive components are the achievement outcomes expected of all students. They are standards of performance and are, therefore, non-negotiable. They appear in the curriculum as goals and objectives. All other components are means, methods, and tools—instruments—to assist in the achievement of goals and objectives. They should be diversified to accommodate different cultural contexts, settings, and clients in the school, community, society, and world. That is, alternative pathways to learning should be used to achieve common performance outcomes in multicultural classrooms. Thus, rationales, content, activities, evaluation procedures, resources, materials, and time lines serve functions in planning for instruction similar to those performed by examples and illustrations in the delivery of teaching. They, too, are conduits through which intended learning becomes personally meaningful to students, and they are the components of curriculum designs most amenable to change.

Without question, all students should learn to read, write, think critically, and solve problems as well as master the disciplinary facts and principles of the subjects commonly taught in schools, such as mathematics, science, social studies, humanities, fine arts, vocational education, and computer literacy. But how they should acquire these skills is less consensual. Answers to this question depend upon whom and what is being taught by whom, as well as when and where the teaching takes place. This means that curriculum content, activities, resources, and performance-appraisal procedures should be varied across and within all domains of learning in order to reflect different ethnic and cultural groups' experiences, contributions, life-styles, and learning-style preferences. Additionally, culturally different literature, arts, and aesthetics should complement factual information; more active learning, participatory partnerships, cooperative arrangements, and creative expressions should be included in learning activities; and more diverse combinations of written, oral, and kinesthetic opportunities should be provided for students to demonstrate task and skill mastery. These kinds of learning experiences are more effective for culturally different students because the content enrichment, varied formats, and multisensory stimulations they offer are more compatible with their cultural values and learning style characteristics.

Classroom Environment

Teaching involves more than creating curriculum designs and engaging in classroom discourse. Another essential component of the process is the physical, social, and interpersonal climates or environments created for learning. According to Rudolf Moos (1979), all classrooms are social environments, and they have several common dimensions: relationships among students and teachers, climate conditions, task orientation, and managerial rules and regulations. Together, these elements form the social context and stage setting for learning.

Research shows that students achieve greater satisfaction, personal growth, and levels of performance in classrooms that include high student involvement, strong personal student-teacher relationships, innovative teaching methods, clarity of rules, affective concern for students as people, and hard work for

51

academic rewards—all within a coherent, well-organized context (Moos 1979). These characteristics are especially significant to learning for culturally different students whose learning styles are field dependent, and whose value orientations are people-centered, affective, humanistic, and group-based. Yet in most U.S. classrooms, students operate largely on an individual basis, have a limited range of movement and involvement, and are expected to function in a rather rigidly organized and sterile physical space. Relationships between students and teachers are formal and somewhat distant, and classroom decorations are too often limited to the mechanical tools (maps, books, machinery, laboratory equipment, and so on) of various subjects areas. The notable exception is elementary classrooms, which tend to be more decorative and where students and teachers work in closer harmony with each other.

Students of some cultural and ethnic groups, especially African Americans, Hispanics, Native Americans, and Native Hawaiians, find "cold," formal, and passive learning environments formidable and disconcerting—so much so that they are distracted from concentrating on academic tasks. Whereas most mainstream schooling procedures use a linear structure (from lining up to enter and exit the classroom, to sitting in straight rows, to serialized participation in discussions, to how information is arranged and presented, to the priority given to individualistic competition), their cultural structures are circular. In learning situations, they prefer group arrangements; integration of affective, cognitive, and psychomotor responses; topic-chaining in the organization and presentation of ideas; and active interaction among all environmental factors (humans, objects, space, and emotional tone). An active and cooperative, warm and emotionally supportive environment is fundamental to their effective learning.

Given the environmental conditions that culturally different students prefer for learning, what are some specific ways in which classroom climates can be modified to embrace more multicultural principles, perspectives, and experiences? Obviously, they will vary somewhat according to the specific setting, circumstances, and people involved. The suggestions offered here serve as guidelines for helping teachers combine their knowledge of classroom-climate components and cultural pluralism to create more effective multicultural learning environments. Possible practices include:

- Using cooperative group, team, and pair arrangements for learning as the normative structure instead of as the occasional exception;
- Using learning stations, multimedia, and interactive video to present information instead of some form of lecturing;
- Varying the format of learning activities frequently to incorporate more affective responses, motion, and movement;
- Establishing friendships between students and teachers;
- Creating genuine partnerships with students so that they are active participants in making decisions about how their learning experiences will occur and be evaluated;
- Changing rules and procedures that govern life in the classroom so they reflect some of the codes of behavior and participation styles of culturally different students;
- Devising ways for students to monitor and manage their own and each other's classroom behaviors;
- Developing an *esprit de corps* of "family" to give cohesion and focused meaning to interpersonal relationships in the classroom;
- Including more human-centered and culturally different images, artifacts, experiences, and incidents in classroom decorations and as props for teaching.

CONCLUSION

The ultimate answer to creating effective instructional practices for multicultural classrooms is empowering teachers to make better decisions for themselves within their own teaching contexts. Empowerment is often interpreted as having the power and authority to make decisions. These are not at issue here. Research clearly and consistently documents the fact that teachers are the power brokers in their classrooms. As John Goodlad's study of schooling shows, the intellectual terrain of the classroom is laid out by teachers, and they play the major role in deciding what, where, when, and how students will learn. Furthermore, teachers at all levels of schooling perceive that they have significant, if not total, control over selecting teaching strategies and learning activities; evaluating students; setting goals and objectives; determining the use of classroom space; scheduling time and materials; grouping students; and selecting content, topics, and skills to be taught. They are virtually autonomous in creating the environment for learning (Goodlad 1984).

Teacher empowerment here means having the knowledge, will, and skill to incorporate cultural pluralism into all routine teaching functions. Having "the knowledge" means understanding how cultural conditioning affects the behaviors of students and teachers, being aware of the cultural contributions of different groups to the various disciplinary domains of knowledge and humankind, and knowing how various teaching tasks converge to form systems of teaching functions. Having "the will" is possessing beliefs and values that accept the legitimacy of cultural differences as well as possessing an enthusiasm to affirm, celebrate, and use these differences to enrich the educational process for all students. Having "the skill" is being competent to translate both new knowledge about multiculturalism and heightened consciousness about the nature of teaching functions into operational strategies that can transform instruction into teaching practices that are more meaningful to a wider variety of students.

The effectiveness of any teaching practices in multicultural classrooms is a direct reflection of how well those aspects that need to be changed are identified and understood. Only then can decisions about *how* to make the necessary changes proceed expeditiously and coherently. Another essential test of effectiveness is the extent to which teaching behaviors combine personal caring with multicultural knowledge and technical competence in working with culturally different students.

While the specific, effective instructional practices for particular multicultural classrooms will vary by setting and circumstance, the analytical, diagnostic, and decision-making processes out of which they emerge are similar for all situations. They include a systems thinking approach to understanding routine teaching tasks and functions, and transforming them so that they incorporate information about and sensitivity to the life experiences, heritages, contributions, and learning styles of students from different ethnic, cultural, racial, and social backgrounds.

REFERENCES

Adams, R.S. 1970. The classroom context. In *Scholars in context: The effects of environments on learning*, edited by W.J. Campbell, 261–83. New York: John Wiley and Sons.

Banks, J.A. 1989. Integrating the curriculum with ethnic content: Approaches and guidelines. In *Multicultural education: Issues and perspectives*, edited by J.A. Banks and C.A. Banks, 189–207. Boston: Allyn and Bacon.

Bennett, C.I. 1990. *Comprehensive multicultural education: Theory and practice.* 2nd ed. Boston: Allyn and Bacon.

Bossert, S.T. 1979. *Tasks and social relationship in classrooms: A study of instructional organization and its consequences.* Cambridge: Harvard University Press.

Cazden, C.B. 1986. Classroom discourse. In *Handbook of research on teaching*, 3rd ed., edited by M.C. Wittrock, 432–63. New York: MacMillan Publishing Co.

Goodlad, J.I. 1984. *A place called school: Prospects for the future.* New York: McGraw-Hill Book Co.

Haysom, J. 1985. *Inquiring into the teaching process: Toward self-evaluation and professional development.* Toronto: Ontario Institute of Studies in Education.

Hudgins, B.B. 1971. *The instructional process.* Chicago: Rand McNally and Co.

Hurt, H.T.; Scott, M.D.; and McCroskey, J.C. 1978. *Communication in the classroom.* Massachusetts: Addison-Wesley Publishing Co.

Jackson, P.W. 1968. *Life in classrooms.* New York: Holt, Rinehart and Winston.

Levy, M.L. 1968. Structural-functional analysis. In *International encyclopedia of the social sciences,* Vol. 6, edited by D.L. Sills, 21–29. New York: The Free Press.

Moos, R.H. 1979. Educational climates. In *Educational environments and effects: Evaluation, policy, and productivity,* edited by H.J. Walberg, 79–100. Berkeley, Calif.: McCutchan Publishing Co.

Rosenshine, B. and Stevens, R. 1986. Teaching functions. In *Handbook of research on teaching,* 3rd ed., edited by M. C. Wittrock, 376–91. New York: MacMillan Publishing Co.

Sleeter, C.E. and Grant, C.A. 1988. *Making choices for multicultural education: Five approaches to race, class, and gender.* Columbus, Oh.: Merrill Publishing Co.

Chapter 4

INSTITUTIONAL CLIMATE: DEVELOPING AN EFFECTIVE MULTICULTURAL SCHOOL COMMUNITY

by Valerie Ooka Pang

> Despair is paralyzing. I urge you to remember that chaotic, distressed, impoverished, and underachieving schools have been turned around by individual efforts, just as our distressed and underachieving students were able to become productive through individual efforts. I am suggesting that most schools and school systems can become more productive and happier places to be than they are right now. Nothing is wrong with public schools that programs to revitalize communities and families cannot improve through participation, cooperation, and an atmosphere of trust (Comer 1980, p.247).

In 1968, Martin Luther King, Jr., Elementary School was one of the lowest-achieving schools in New Haven, Connecticut (Comer 1988). The school was 99 percent black, and more than 70 percent of the students received Aid for Dependent Children. The school had serious discipline and attendance problems. Its students and their parents felt frustrated with and alienated from the school. And its teachers were depressed and exhausted from trying to cope within a hostile environment. But, miraculously, by 1980 students were performing above the national average in math and reading, and the attendance rate was one of the best in the district.

How did these successes occur? During 1968, the school became the focal point of university consultants, administrators, teachers, parents, and students. As these groups joined forces and discussions evolved, everyone became hopeful, and this hope transferred into commitment. Administrators, teachers, parents, and students began working together with the common vision that all children have enormous potential and that all children can reach their potential. Those students and parents who once felt frustrated and alienated became actively involved in the learning process; students, in particular, challenged their teachers and themselves to know more. Teachers, in turn, rose to the challenges.

The purpose of this chapter is to focus upon the question: What are the factors that create a successful multicultural school, one where students from diverse populations exhibit competence in basic skills and where the total school environment reflects cultural diversity?

THE INSTITUTIONAL CLIMATE

Numerous factors contribute to an overall climate of either hope or despair in schools. School is a place where many social phenomena, such as ethnicity, economic level, and gender, meet and interact. Children may come from families that have little money, speak a language other than English, and/or have behaviors and values that differ from those of middle-class schools. District policies, school practices, faculty makeup, curriculum content, instructional strategies, and school routines may force these students to choose between cultural identity and school success. This distressing dilemma can cause them to suffer from depression, frustration, and confusion. (Fordham, 1988). In addition, school faculties may suffer from low morale, lack of respect, and a heavily burdened curriculum that requires them to deal with issues such as nuclear war, AIDS, drug abuse, teenage pregnancies, and day-care of young children.

To create successful multicultural schools, learning must be seen from an entire-system approach that: (1) promotes respect for and forges cooperation of all community-school personnel, and (2) reflects cultural diversity in its curriculum and instructional programs.

Successful characteristics of multicultural schools should not be perceived as a shopping list of research-proven factors that can be selected from the shelf, purchased, and then used. Educators and parents must engage in discussions about their vision for their school and how these characteristics work simultaneously to support a "can-do" school climate.

Before even examining these characteristics, one must recognize six important factors about the research on effective schools.

First, effective-school research literature includes studies of both high-middle class, white schools and of poor, culturally diverse schools. Initially, James Coleman was commissioned to conduct a national study of equality of educational opportunity in 1965. His research found that family background was a large determinant of school success. Many educators interpreted this to mean that schools did not have much impact on the learning process (Coleman 1966).

More recently, however, the literature on effective schools has shifted, and professionals have adopted the belief that schools can teach all children (Cohen 1987). One of the pioneers in this research was Ronald Edmonds. His studies focused attention on successful schools that served poor, culturally diverse schools. He believed that once he identified common characteristics of these successful schools, it would be possible to transfer those elements to schools that were failing their students (Edmonds 1979).

Research on thriving, culturally diverse schools centers on building supportive school communities. There is a strong sense of "we" in these schools. The collaborative effort of teachers, parents, and students working together as responsible, interdependent allies builds an educational climate that offers a predictable, encouraging, and supportive environment (Comer 1980).

Second, because schools are like people, one must recognize that every school has individual strengths and needs. Something that may be exceptionally successful at one school may only be moderately effective in another. In reviewing the components that correlate with school success, one should remember that there is no single recipe for a healthy learning ecology. The culture of each school may differ not only in ethnicity, but also in social class, rural or urban setting, and language groups. Schools will journey toward school success on different roads and in different vehicles.

Third, one must be aware that though much of the professional literature points to correlations between various components, it does not explain cause-and-effect relationships based within well-defined theoretical models. This can limit the applicability of some effective schools literature (Comer, Haynes, and Hamilton Lee 1987–88).

Fourth, although research has provided important information about school reform, the quantitative examination of successful schools often ignores intangible and other hidden factors that contribute to achievement. They do not explore the following questions: How are working interpersonal relationships formed between teacher and parent? Between student and parent? Between teacher and administrator? How can the cultural background of students be integrated into the curriculum and instruction of schools? How do teachers acknowledge and value the life-styles that students bring to schools? How are cultural diversities seen in schools, as deficits or differences? (The differing ways in which teachers, administrators, and parents view these questions will also have definite impact upon the climate of schools.)

Fifth, one must recognize that schools are important social organizations. Schools tend to reflect mainstream values in their structures, curriculum, and interactions. The historically reinforced stratifications of American society, which are based upon level of wealth, social status, and student ethnicity, often are seen as principal determinants of school success (Wilson and Fergus 1988). School staff members should examine their own values and beliefs about student potential in light of these orientations. Do school members operate from a belief that students from low-income, culturally diverse communities are not as capable as those from affluent, white neighborhoods? Some school staff members reinforce the social status by mirroring an overall atmosphere of schools as places where teachers "know best" about schooling and parents should not interfere in the process. Also, there are parents who send their children to school with comments like, "You don't have to listen to the teacher." This mindset may have developed from negative experiences parents had when they were in school. These attitudes will not contribute to the development of a cohesive school community.

And sixth, the movement toward effective school research, in part, represents a strong corporate agenda found in today's schools. Many of the tools that have been brought forth in school reform reflect an organizational and management orientation. Though these tools can strengthen the school structure, schools should not be equated with factories or offices. Schools are unique institutions whose purpose is to develop fulfilled, responsible citizens who are active participants in a democratic society (Goodlad 1984).

While schools want graduates to be economically self-sufficient, their principle function is not strictly to produce workers for business. The complexity of the relationship between business and schools is due in part to the assumption that the underlying economic infrastructure of society is dependent on schools to produce workers for business. Yet, if schools see their mission as preparing responsible citizens, there may be a vast difference in purpose between schools and business. Schools are not profit-driven and do not view students as commodities being produced or managed. Transferring what works in a factory or office may not always be suitable for schools.

CHARACTERISTICS THAT FOSTER SUCCESSFUL SCHOOLS

The research on effective schools has been uneven, and

definitions of success vary. Yet specific characteristics emerge that seem to impact healthy school climate and academic achievement (Murphy 1989). The following such characteristics will be discussed as key to the implementation of successful schools in diverse communities:

1. The school community engages in lengthy discussions about curriculum, organizational structure, assessment instruments, and educational purpose.
2. The school community believes in the ability of all students to succeed, and this vision permeates all areas of school.
3. Parents are participating partners in schools.
4. Teachers are involved in the decision-making process.
5. The principal is a key leader in guiding and directing the collective effort of the learning community.
6. Instruction is founded on developmental and social-skill needs of students.
7. Teachers consistently monitor and reinforce student academic performance.

School Community Dialogue

Establishing dialogue between parents and school faculty as well as between faculty member and faculty member is an important first stage in constructing a cohesive school community. These ongoing, continuous discussions create trusting, interpersonal relationships among parents, teachers, and administrators, which, in turn, lead to shared vision and effective decision-making. Through this process, consistent role models at home and school develop and reinforce similar academic, behavioral, and social expectations.

Teachers who have the opportunity to discuss concerns and problems with each other are more likely to develop supportive professional networks. By sharing ideas and effective instructional approaches to curriculum and discipline problems, teachers minimize individual isolation. Moreover, dialogue with parents can help to develop understanding and support for school programs. Parents become better informed about the kinds of pressures teachers face, and how they can aid teachers as volunteers and as role models at home.

High Expectations

Successful schools possess high expectations for all students. Often students from culturally diverse communities have been told through overt and covert avenues that they are not as good as white students, that they will not do well because of their background. They overhear teachers say things like, "Well, you can't expect anything from these children. Their parents don't care, and they come from transient families." After a while, children internalize these attitudes and begin to believe them. For children who are members of a disenfranchised minority group that has historically been victimized by society, this message is almost insidious (Comer 1980). Teachers must reinforce the belief that all students can achieve by conveying high expectations.

One way teachers convey high expectations to students is through teacher-interactional patterns (Cohen 1987). Teachers wait longer for responses from high-achieving students and respond to their questions more often. They also give them more praise and extensive feedback because they expect high achievement.

One way that schools reinforce low expectations is through ability-group techniques. Though many teachers believe that these grouping methods are the most effective means of instruction, Robert Slavin has found that ability grouping is not more effective than heterogeneous placement of students, and that grouping has the most negative effects upon lower-track pupils because it reduces their expectations (Slavin et al. 1989). Alternatives to traditional ability-grouping practices are beginning to be developed that should change the way students see themselves and the manner in which teachers deal with academic and cultural diversity. They will enhance school climate by: (1) conveying the belief that all students can reach their enormous potentials, and (2) developing instructional practices and curriculum that reinforce that vision.

Parent/Community Involvement

Parents are children's first teachers and most important role models (Herenton 1987). Unfortunately, they often do not know how the educational process operates or how they can participate in it in a way that will help their children. Schools can solicit effective community and parent participation in two major ways: by recruiting parents to become involved in everyday school activities and by eliciting a broad-based community effort in the educational enterprise.

James Comer and his colleagues designed the School Development Program in New Haven, Connecticut, specifically to promote active parent-involvement in schools. The Comer schools instituted three levels of parent participation. The first level was broad-based participation in which parents were invited to whole-school activities, such as potluck suppers, gospel music nights, and general meetings. These events served as bridges between home and school. The second level involved participation in day-to day school affairs and brought parents into the classrooms to work as assistants and tutors. Some parents became volunteers and others received minimum wage for about 15 hours of employment. The third level supported parent participation in school governance. It aimed "to develop patterns of shared responsibility and decision making among parents and staff" (Comer 1980, p. 68). The schools encouraged parents to act as partners in schooling rather than as separate advisors. Teachers, principals, and members of the Comer team trained these parents in intervention, developmental, and instructional strategies.

This model has been extremely successful. Students at Martin Luther King, Jr., and Katharine Brennan Elementary Schools in New Haven from 1969 through 1984 produced continual gains in math and reading scores (Comer 1988, p. 47). When the project first began, these schools ranked lowest in achievement among the district's 33 schools. By 1984, the fourth-grade students were found to be third and fourth in the district on the Iowa Test of Basic Skills. In addition, the attendance rates became some of the best in the city, and behavior problems declined drastically. Comer believed that the success of the program was due to their *ethos*, or structured approach of collaborative decision-making, rather than defining school climate in terms of rules, discipline, or teacher expectations (Comer, Haynes, and Hamilton-Lee 1987–88, p. 196). Parents were key to their effective school model.

Another successful avenue for encouraging parental involvement is the community-based approach. The Rochester Education Initiative, designed by the Urban League, fostered a grassroots program to inform the community of the low achievement of Black students and the need for a holistic and community-organized program to address the serious educational needs of young people (Johnson, Dwyer, and Spade 1987–88). The League received assistance from businesses, churches, human services, and governmental agencies in developing a comprehensive educational plan.

The project began with public forums that featured speakers from educator, student, and parent groups. These speakers addressed the key question: "What can we do to improve the academic performance of Rochester's students?" Later, community leaders conducted town meetings where educators and community representatives formed school-action committees to develop a range of school improvement projects that included job incentives for student achievement, a marketing program that highlighted the importance of education, and management expertise from the business sector.

The early stages of the plan showed improvement in student-achievement levels for African American ninth, tenth, and eleventh graders. In particular, the number of those students who had B or higher grade averages increased from 226 students in 1986 to 346 in 1987 (Johnson, Dwyer, and Spade 1987–1988, p. 226).

Teacher Involvement in Decision Making

Teachers comprise the largest segment of school faculty, yet often they may not be involved in important school decisions. Successful schools have the participation of the total faculty in planning and executing school reform. In the Comer project, teacher representatives were elected to the school's governance and management team (Comer 1988). This team examined school curriculum and structure and its relationship to student behavior and academic performance. Though the principal was an authority figure, he/she considered the input of this team before making decisions. Major decisions were made by consensus because Comer and his colleagues felt shared decision making resulted in a broader feeling of ownership.

Effective Leadership of the Principal

Principals are key leaders in developing bridges of communication among staff, students, and community. Effective principals understand and view instruction from a system-wide perspective. They can clearly articulate the goals of their schools and can integrate policy into practice by using shared decision making with teachers and parents.

Understanding learning from an ecological perspective, effective principals create mechanisms for dialogue and rapport in which parents and teachers develop a sense of ownership that supports the learning process (Comer 1980, pp. 233–235). Additionally, these principals provide administrative support for community decisions about schooling. They often have financial and human resources that can assist in funding structural and innovative changes (Wilson and Firestone 1987).

Focus on Developmental and Social Skills

Successful schools create instructional programs that focus on both cognitive and social-skill development.

Educators in these schools do not perceive their students as empty vessels, but as active learners (Devaney and Sykes 1988). They know that rote facts and worksheets will not prepare students to tackle social problems; they know that they must find better ways to develop the critical-thinking skills needed to do so—and they do. These teachers can move from their reliance on textbooks and prepackaged materials to active investigation of social problems connected to students' lives (Goodlad 1984). They know that meaningful relationships between curriculum and life need to be built; otherwise, schools will be removed from reality.

A curriculum that is relevant to the daily lives of students also helps build positive school climate (Firestone and Rosenblum 1988). High school students, in particular, often seek connections between the curriculum and the many personal judgments and decisions that they make. For example, students want to know how learning U.S. history is going to have any bearing upon their ability to earn money or make important decisions. They are more motivated to learn when school content considers their life situations.

In one instance, a group of students requested that their high school examine the underlying issues of racism found at school. They successfully organized a series of school-wide discussions on racism and instituted a pilot course on human behavior that included a large unit on racism. As a result of these activities, the students were able to present school administrators with a list of recommendations for structural changes in the curriculum and in district policies that would address racial problems in their school (Polakow-Suransky and Neda Ulaby

1990). Their actions are an example of how students can force schools to make their education more relevant to the social conflicts that exist in their lives.

In a positive climate for learning, children also have social skills that reinforce the education process. For example, teachers may have helped them develop skills that support cooperative-learning activities, risk taking, and positive interpersonal interactions.

Regular Monitoring of Student Progress and Reinforcement of Success

Successful schools institute monitoring programs that measure student achievement and performance. These schools are constantly assessing their own effectiveness as well, because the data they gather on student performance helps them identify their own areas of weakness. Some schools have instituted criterion-referenced tests for evaluating student progress, which helps teachers to continually check students' knowledge levels in basic skill areas, reinforce successes, and adjust instruction accordingly (Firestone 1989). By making students accountable for their learning, teachers create an environment that reflects high expectations.

CONCLUSION

We have too many at-risk schools, institutions that are struggling to serve our diverse student population. Instead, we need more risking schools, institutions that challenge themselves to create new structures; ones that allow for the infusion of content and strategies that are effective with a diverse student population.

Building a school community is central to the academic and social success of all students. Children often attend schools miles from their homes; in such cases, it may be impossible to build a communal sense with the surrounding neighborhood. Yet it is conceivable to create a community of caring adults made up of teachers, administrators, parents, and other community role models. In creating that community, school personnel must make the curriculum relevant to students' daily lives.

Cultural and class background may be pivotal elements in the community from which students come. Unfortunately, literature on effective schools offers scattered findings or little research that focuses on the impact of cultural context on the school environment. Cultural factors may not be easily quantified into existing models of school reform. While separate school programs may not be needed for inner-city and suburban schools, there is no one model for school success. Though massive data bases have been gathered on multicultural education, the intangible effect of culture on the psycho-social development of students often is overlooked. Securing parent involvement, using education materials relevant to the community life of students, and understanding that students' motivational system may have cultural roots can help build strong self-concepts.

When educators do not understand how school values and behaviors may conflict with community life-styles, students face the dilemma of choosing between their cultural identity and fitting in at school; these students can suffer from depression, frustration, and confusion. Schools need to understand that the social-cultural context of learning has a major impact upon the interactions and structure of present-day schooling. When schools deny the role of culture and social-political status in the hidden and stated curriculum, the learning environment cannot provide students with an equal educational opportunity.

The process of multicultural schooling is complicated. Educational equity can only occur when we make courageous systemic school changes. We face tremendous problems in schools today; among these are resegregated patterns of student population, escalating dropouts rates, and the continued growth of the underclass. To deal with these problems effectively, we must continue to strengthen the relationship between ethnic communities and schools through dialogue, collective goal setting, and action planning. For ultimately, all children can be successful in schools.

REFERENCES

Cohen, M. 1987. Improving school effectiveness: Lessons from research. In *Educator's handbook*, edited by V. Richardson-Koehler, 474–490. New York: Longman Publishers.

Coleman, J. 1966. *Equality of educational opportunity.* Washington, DC: U.S. Office of Education.

Comer, J. 1988. Educating poor minority children. *Scientific American* 259 (5): 42–28.

Comer, J. 1980. *School power.* New York: The Free Press.

Comer, J.; Haynes, N.; and Hamilton-Lee, M. 1987–1988. School power: A model for improving black student achievement. *Urban Review* 11(1–2):187–200

Devaney, K. and Sykes, G. 1988. Making the case for professionalism. In *Building a professional culture in schools*, edited by A. Lieberman, 3–22. New York: Teachers College Press.

Edmonds, R. 1979. Some schools work and more can. *Social Policy* 9: 28–32

Educational Record. 1987-88. The Boston compact fosters city-wide collaboration. Fall 1987–Winter 1988: 51.

Firestone, W.A. 1989. Beyond order and expectations in high schools serving at-risk youth. *Educational Leadership* 46 (5): 45.

Firestone, W.A. and Rosenblum, S. 1988. Building commitment in urban high schools. *Educational Evaluation and Policy Analysis* 10 (4): 285–99.

Fordham, S. 1988. Racelessness as a factor in black students' school success: Pragmatic strategy or pyrrhic victory? *Harvard Educational Review* 58 (1): 54–84.

Goodlad, J.I. 1984 *A place called school.* New York: McGraw-Hill Book Company.

Herenton, W. 1987–1988. Memphis inner-city school improvement project: A holistic approach for developing academic excellence. *Urban Review* 11 (1–2): 211–26

Johnson, W.A.; Dwyer, B.; and Spade, J.Z. 1987–1988. A community initiative: Making a difference in the quality of black education. *Urban Review* 11 (1–2): 217–26.

Murphy, J. 1989. Educational reform in the 1980s: Explaining some surprising success. *Educational Evaluation and Policy Analysis* 11 (3): 209–21.

Polakow-Suransky, S. and Ulaby, N. 1990. Students take action to combat racism. *Phi Delta Kappan* 71 (8): 601–06.

Slavin, R.E.; Braddock, J.H.; Hall, C.; and Petza, R. J. Alternatives to ability grouping. John Hopkins University, June 1989. Research funded by a grant from the National Education Association.

Wilson, B.L. and Firestone, W.A. 1987. The principal and instruction: Combining bureaucratic and cultural linkages. *Educational Leadership* 45 (1): 18–23.

Wilson, C.D. and Fergus, E.O. 1988. Combining effective schools and school improvement research traditions for achieving equity-based education. *Equity and Excellence* 24 (1): 54–65.

Chapter 5

LEARNING STYLES: IMPLICATIONS FOR TEACHERS

by Karen Swisher

Ten years ago in a publication by the National Education Association, Barbara Cox and Manuel Ramirez (1981) asked the following questions:

> Do minority students have a "style of learning" that is different from mainstream students? Are minority students really any different from other students in the way they learn? If such differences do exist, how have they developed? What can or should educators do to be responsive to these differences? (p. 61).

Their questions and similar questions posed by other educational researchers and practitioners continue to be compelling ones as we prepare to enter the twenty-first century. The search for more effective ways to serve an increasing number of students who have not been well-served by our nation's schools has never been more important than it is now. The "browning of America" is giving our schools a different complexion; the number of children who live below the poverty line and/or are homeless is increasing; and the high number of "at-risk" or "school-weary" students has caused alarm. All of these factors are reported among the many concerns in the call for reforming or restructuring American schools.

The purpose of this chapter is to focus on the construct of learning styles as a promising, yet not "panaceaistic," view of successful schooling for our multicultural population of students. Knowledge about learning styles has recently been more accessible to practitioners. "In the last decade, some teachers have begun to experiment with *learning styles*, persuaded that the concept helps them to both understand differences better and to provide for those differences, thereby improving learning" (Brandt 1990, p. 3). It goes without saying that some expert teachers have intuitively been doing this for years. They have always accommodated students' individual differences by varying their style of instruction or by giving students options for demonstrating competence. This chapter is intended to validate the convictions and spirit of those expert teachers and to provide information for those who want to know more, recognizing that "we continue to do our best, knowing that we don't know everything, but keeping our minds open to the emerging knowledge that can help us be more effective" (Brandt 1990, p. 3).

LEARNING STYLES DEFINED

The definition of *learning style* has been discussed and debated for several years. In 1983, the National Task Force on Learning Style and Brain Behavior offered the following definition:

> *Learning style* is that consistent pattern of behavior and performance by which an individual approaches educational experiences. It is the composite of characteristic cognitive, affective, and physiological behaviors that serve as relatively stable indicators of how a learner perceives, interacts with, and responds to the learning environment. It is formed in the deep structure of neural organization and personality [that] molds and is molded by human development and the cultural experiences of home, school, and society (Keefe and Langios, p. 1).

This definition, with emphasis on "cultural experiences of home, school, and society," is the basis for the following discussion of learning styles and its implications for teaching and learning in a multicultural society.

RESEARCH BASE

Research into the nature of learning styles began decades ago. Using tests of perception, Herman Witkin and his associates

73

in 1954 began to study the field-dependent and field-independent dimension of cognitive style. Their work was concerned with how people use the visual environment around them; in other words, the extent to which the surrounding organized field influences the person's perception of an item within it. For example, in an embedded-figures test, participants were asked to locate a simple figure in a more complex pattern. Individual differences in performance indicated some people were able to quickly locate the simple figure; they saw the items as separate from the surrounding field and were designated field independent. Those who could not locate the figure in the time allotted were designated field dependent because their perception was dominated by the surrounding field.

Field-independent learners have a perception of discrete parts and are good at abstract analytical thought. They tend to be individualistic, less sensitive to the emotions of others, and have poorly developed social skills. They favor inquiry and independent study and can provide their own structure to facilitate learning. Field-independent learners are intrinsically motivated and less responsive to social reinforcement.

Conversely, field-dependent learners have a global perspective and are less adept at analytical problem solving. They tend to be highly sensitive and attuned to the social environment; their social skills are highly developed. They favor a spectator approach to learning and organize information to be learned in the form it is given. They are extrinsically motivated and responsive to social reinforcement (Witkin et al. 1967).

Several researchers have applied other names to describe the ends of the cognitive style continuum. For example, Rosalie Cohen (1969) described the dimensions as analytical and relational. Ramirez and Alfredo Castañeda (1974) believed that the term "dependent" implied negative connotations and substituted the term "sensitive" in its place, thus "field sensitive" and "field independent" are terms identified with their work.

RELATIONSHIP BETWEEN CULTURE AND LEARNING STYLES

The relationship between culture and cognitive style, as conceptualized by Witkin and others, has been studied over the last two decades. For example, Ramirez and Castañeda (1974) built upon the research of Witkin (1967), which indicated that socialization practices play a large role in determining learning behavior preferences in children. A framework set forth by Ramirez and Castañeda in 1974 suggests that cultural values influence socialization practices (1981), which affect the ways children prefer to learn. Cox and Ramirez (1981) explained the framework in this way:

> Clearly, the task, the situation, and the materials influence the ways that children are encouraged to learn or behave, and few families encourage only field-independent or field-sensitive learning, even though on the average they may use one type of strategy more than the other. The predominant or general teaching style of a family may thus be of basic importance in deciding the direction a child's learning preferences may take. Insofar as these teaching styles reflect a certain set of values held by parents and family, values that in many cases are clearly culturally determined, one may posit that cultural differences in learning-style preferences develop through children's early experiences. (p. 63)

Differences in socialization practices in Mexican American, African American, Asian American, and American Indian and Alaskan Native cultures suggest that a model such as the one presented by Ramirez and Castañeda has credence. For example, if sharing, generosity, and cooperation are respected cultural values, children will be socialized accordingly, and their approach to learning may reflect a preference for shared-group learning or decision making rather than for independent learning.

While there is evidence of the relationship between culture and learning styles, there is also great concern that characterizing learners from particular cultural backgrounds as having a specific learning style may result in discriminatory practice or excuses for failure. However, schools in general have expected learning styles to be more analytical or field independent, and some learners whose styles may be more relational or field dependent/sensitive have not done well in our schools. Other students have changed and adapted very well, lending support to the notion that styles are learned. But learners should not have to bear sole responsibility for adapting or changing; schools can and should share it.

MULTICULTURAL EDUCATION AND LEARNING STYLES

The ideology of a culturally pluralistic society in which the diversity of populations is given equal recognition and value was recognized and expressed in the philosophy of "the original proud possessors of this continent" who were cognizant of the diversity "not only of the winged peoples of the air, but also, the two-leggeds—humankind." (Whiteman et al. 1974, p. 197). In the early twentieth century, philosopher Horace Kallen (1924) reaffirmed this right in the concept we know as cultural pluralism. In our nation's schools, multicultural education is the embodiment of this concept.

Multicultural education recognizes that there are multiple ways of perceiving, evaluating, believing, and behaving. We recognize that people perceive and learn about the world in different ways, and that they demonstrate this understanding in unique ways. How they have learned to learn about their world is characteristic of the socialization practices within the cultures from which they come. While we can articulate the importance of this concept, we are still not very good at determining what this means in terms of providing education that is multicultural. Thus, we believe it has to do with providing each child an equal opportunity to develop to full potential; we understand that attending to individual differences may mean treating children unequally; and we prefer to talk about treating children equitably

76

and fairly rather than equally or the same. The learning-styles construct is a vehicle for doing what Christine Bennett (1990) has suggested, that is, moving us beyond the rhetoric associated with individual differences and educational equity.

LEARNING STYLE DIFFERENCES

An awareness of the characteristics of groups of people is important. We must also realize that this knowledge helps us to understand groups, not individual learners. Diversity within each cultural or ethnic group exists and is demonstrated in aspects such as language use, child-rearing practices, and socialization methods. Diversity is also determined by the degree to which members of a particular group have assimilated aspects of the larger society or macroculture and the social class to which the family "belongs." Because of this intragroup diversity, it is unrealistic to think that all members of a certain group will have a particular learning style. However, there are general characteristics that provide a basis for further investigation into the individual characteristics that constitute style. Presenting information about the learning styles of African Americans, American Indians and Alaskan Natives, Asian Americans, and Hispanics may contribute to greater understanding, but it may also reinforce stereotypical notions about the relationship between learning styles and cultural group membership. It is with this caution that the following information is presented.

African Americans

Researchers such as Janice Hale-Benson (1986), Asa Hilliard (1976), and Barbara Shade (1982) have focused on the learning styles of African American youth. They have noted differences between African American students and their multicultural counterparts as well as differences among African American students themselves. Hale-Benson and Hilliard, for example, have used the work of Cohen (1969) in describing African American youth as more relational than analytical in their approach to learning. *Relational* is similar to Witkin's field-dependent conceptual style and is produced by family socialization patterns in which members share functions, thereby socializing their members to be more relational in their learning styles. Shade suggested that success in school requires sequential, analytical, or object-oriented cognitive styles; the "culture or life-style and world view of Afro-Americans, however, portrays strategies designed to foster survival and therefore tends to be rather universalistic, intuitive, and more than that, very person-oriented" (Shade 1982).

American Indians and Alaskan Natives

What do we know about the learning styles of American Indian and Alaskan Native children who come from more than 500 tribal groups? We have very little empirical data available when one considers that as an indigenous group, American Indians are among the most researched of all cultures in this country.

A review of the literature regarding American Indian learning styles by Karen Swisher and D. Deyhle (1989) presented some anecdotal and empirical information from various researchers about several tribal groups. Similarities exist, perhaps because of the indigenous nature shared by all groups, but there are differences as well. For example, Navajo, Oglala Sioux, and Yaqui cultures teach that competence should precede performance. Observation and self-testing in private are important steps that must be taken before one demonstrates competence of a task. The review also cited the visual strengths of Kwakuitl and Eskimo children of the Northwest and of Navajo and Pueblo children of the Southwest as well as the cooperative nature of Cherokee and Kwakuitl children.

Gaining communicative competence and participation in classroom interactional structures were areas studied by Susan Philips (1983) in her work with Indian children in Warm Springs, Oregon. She found that community norms as well as socialization practices had greatly influenced the way children gained communicative competence and their preference for participation in small cooperative-learning groups. It has been speculated that American Indians tend to be field dependent; however, recent exploratory work on learning styles of Jicarilla Apache children by Swisher and Bonnie Page (1990) indicated that intragroup differences exist to the point that no general tendencies could be determined.

Asian Americans

Intragroup diversity among Asian Americans is often overlooked in favor of a recent characterization of Asians as the "model minority." Asian students have been typified as hard working, high achieving, polite, and docile. This style of learning appears to be compatible with what is expected in American classrooms; therefore, research into this dimension of their educational experience has been limited. While we know that the same spectrum of diversity is found in the Asian American group as in other minorities, the experiences of recent immigrants from Southeast Asia serve as a vivid reminder of that fact. Differences in child-rearing and socialization practices, language, and communication in the families from which the children come should alert us to diversity in learning styles. We should not make assumptions based on behavioral observations. Additional information on the myths and stereotypes of Asian Americans and recent Southeast Asian newcomers are provided by the works of Valerie Ooka Pang (1990) and of Don Nakanishi and Marsha Hirano-Nakanishi (1983).

Hispanics

Hispanic is a term that encompasses people from Spanish-speaking ancestry, nations, or territories, regardless of race. But they are all people with different histories. Heterogeneity characterizes this large group of Spanish-speaking people, although they do share some religious, social, and cultural values.

The landmark work of Ramirez and Castañeda on learning styles of Mexican American children has provided a definitive lens through which the relationship between culture and learning can be viewed. Their framework, described earlier in this chapter, suggested that socialization practices influenced by cultural values strongly affect the ways in which children approach learning tasks. Their research indicated that Mexican American children tend to be field sensitive in their learning styles. For example, they prefer to work with others to achieve a common goal, and they tend to be more sensitive to the feelings and opinions of others (Ramirez and Castañeda1974).

A Final Note

Having said that "minority students may more often display preferences for field-sensitive learning approaches," Cox and Ramirez (1981) caution us to not ignore the great diversity within any culture. They remind us that the learning-styles construct should be a tool for individualization, rather than a label for categorizing and evaluating.

IMPLICATIONS FOR PRACTICE

What does the information contained in this chapter imply? First of all, it suggests that "educational equity will exist for all students when teachers become sensitive to the cultural diversity in their classrooms, vary their teaching styles so as to appeal to a diverse student population, and modify their curricula to include ethnic content (Banks).

Swisher and Deyhle (1989) propose that teachers who are empathetic and want to change, do not do so simply because they have not had the time to reflect, research, and restructure their teaching style. There may never be enough time to do this, but it is an essential element in understanding the learning styles of all children in our classrooms. Several informal and formal guides have been developed for identification of learning styles. Getting to know our students and their home background should be a requisite beginning-of-the-year activity. Bennett encourages teachers to, first of all, know their own learning and teaching styles and then determine how far they can comfortably stray from these strengths and preferences. She cautions teachers to build classroom flexibility slowly, adding one new strategy at a time. She encourages teachers to consider all modes of instruction (visual, auditory, tactile, and kinesthetic) when teaching new concepts and skills. Multisensory approaches should be an important consideration in all instructional delivery.

In the 1981 NEA publication, *Education in the '80s: Implications for Multiethnic Education*, Cox and Ramirez suggested a process for assessment and planning. The suggestions are still very practical for teachers to consider:

1. Assess students' preferred ways of learning and the way(s) in which student behaviors change from situation to situation.

2. Plan learning experiences that address conceptual goals or skills or other objectives that incorporate the student's preferred ways of learning by using teaching methods, incentives, materials, and situations that are planned according to student preferences.

3. Implement the learning experiences that were planned.

4. Evaluate the learning experiences in terms of attainment of conceptual or other goals as well as in terms of observed student behaviors and involvement.

5. As the year progresses, plan and implement student participation in learning experiences that require behaviors the student has previously avoided. Incorporate only one aspect at a time of the total experience from the less familiar behaviors—focusing on only the reward, the materials, the situation,

or the task requirements—so that the student uses what is familiar and comfortable or motivating as support for the newer learning experience aspects.

6. Continue to provide familiar, comfortable, successful experiences as well as to gradually introduce the children to learning new ways (pp. 64–65).

Informal student and teacher observable behavior checklists have been developed by Ramirez and Castañeda (1974); they provide valuable tools in the identification of both learning and teaching-style tendencies. Other instruments that assess cognitive style, affective style, perceptual modality, and multidimensional aspects have been developed and are described in a publication by Claudia Cornett (1983).

CONCLUSION

Knowledge about learning styles is a powerful component in a teacher's repertoire of effective instruction. Use or implementation of knowledge about learning styles demonstrates, in an observable manner, the valuing of diversity. The fundamental values of equity, fairness, and equal treatment of all children are manifested in teachers' personal behaviors as they adapt their instruction and interact with learners. Above all, knowledge about the learning-style characteristics of particular groups should be used as a guide, not a stereotype, for understanding individuals in our schools. While not conclusive, there is evidence that achievement is affected by teaching to students' learning-style strengths.

REFERENCES

Banks, J.A. 1988. Ethnicity, class, cognitive, and motivational styles: Research and training implications. *Journal of Negro Education* 57 (4): 466.

Bennett, C. 1990. *Comprehensive multicultural education*. Boston: Allyn and Bacon.

Brandt, R. 1990. If we only knew enough. *Educational Leadership* 48 (2): 3.

Cohen, R.A. 1969. Conceptual styles, cultural conflict, and nonverbal tests of intelligence. *American Anthropologist* 71: 828–56.

Cornett, C.E. 1983. *What you should know about teaching and learning styles.* Bloomington, Id.: Phi Delta Kappan Foundation.

Cox, B.G. and Ramirez, M. 1981. Cognitive styles: Implications for multiethnic education. In *Education in the '80s: Implications for multiethnic education,* edited by J. A. Banks, 61. Washington, DC: National Education Association.

Hale-Benson, J.E. 1986. *Black children: Their roots, culture, and learning styles.* Revised ed. Baltimore, Md.: The John Hopkins University Press.

Hilliard, A. 1976. Alternatives to IQ testing: An approach to the identification of gifted minority children. Final report to the California State Department of Education, 1976.

Kallen, H.M. 1924. *Culture and democracy in the United States.* New York: Boni and Liveright.

Keefe, J.W. and Languis, M. 1983. *Learning Stages Network Newsletter* 4 (2): 1.

Nakanishi, D.T. and Hirano-Nakanishi, M. eds. 1983. *The education of Asian and Pacific American: Historical perspectives and prescriptions for the future.* Phoenix, Az.: Oryx Press.

Pang, V.O. 1990. Asian-American children: A diverse population. *The Education Forum* 55: 49–66.

Philips, S.U. 1983. *The invisible culture.* New York: Longman Publishers.

Ramirez, M. and Castañeda, A. 1974. *Cultural democracy, bicognitive development, and education.* New York: Academic Press.

Shade, B.J. 1982. Afro-American cognitive style: A variable in school success? *Review of Educational Research* 52 (2): 219–44.

Swisher, K. and Deyhle, D. 1989. The styles of learning are different, but teaching is just the same: Suggestions for teachers of American Indian youth. *Journal of American Indian Education,* August 1989, 1–14.

Swisher, K. and Page, B. 1990. Determining Jicarilla Apache learning styles: A collaborative approach. Paper delivered at the Annual Meeting of the American Educational Research Association, Boston, Mass., 18 April 1990.

Whiteman, H.; Covington, R.J.; Holland, F.; Lemon, D.; and Locke, P. 1974. The Native American perspective on teacher competencies: It is not necessary for eagles to be crows. In *Multicultural education through competency-based teacher education*, edited by W.A. Hunter, p. 197. Washington, DC: American Association of Colleges of Teacher Education

Witkin, H.A. 1967. A cognitive style approach to cross-cultural research. *International Journal of Psychology* 2: 233–50.

Witkin, H.A.; Moore, C.A.; Goodenough, D.R.; and Cox, P.W. 1977. *Cognitive style and the teaching/learning process.* Cassette series 3F. Washington, DC: American Educational Research Association.

Chapter 6

RETHINKING THE ROLE OF GENDER AND ACHIEVEMENT IN SCHOOLING

by Jane Bernard-Powers

Michelle, a 12-year-old girl whom I know very well, recently reminded me of a powerful stereotype that emerges in early adolescence and shadows young women through their high school years. She said that "brainy" girls are not popular. Just as Carl Grant and Christine Sleeter (1986) found at Five Bridges Junior High School in their study entitled "After the School Bell Rings," cultural imperatives about gender roles are still part of the fabric of school life. The tenaciously low enrollment figures for young women in advanced mathematics and physics courses, the dominance of young men participating in industrial arts courses and high-school athletics, and persisting evidence of textbook bias all serve to remind educators of the significance of gender in schools (Fanner and Sidney 1985).

This chapter explores the influence of gender, that is, the significance of being male or female on educational experiences and achievement. It begins with an introduction to current theoretical issues on sex differences and then discusses gender biases in testing, content areas, and classroom management.

THEORETICAL CONSIDERATIONS

The connections between life opportunities, achievement in schools, and gender dynamics seem self-evident. However, the last 20 years of scholarship, informed reflection, and research have taught us that specific causal relationships are elusive and that gender dynamics in schools are complex. Early attempts to solve "the problem" of sexism in schools focused on

85

equity and documentation of differences. *Equity* was a key concept that came to mean fairness in the distribution of funding and human resources, access to courses and curriculum materials that reflected the range of human experiences, and the elimination of gender stereotypes that demeaned females and limited males. Two decades after the equity report "Dick and Jane as Victims" was published, it is clear that identifying and documenting the problems of sexism were only the first critical steps, and that the simple refurbishing of an earlier cupboard cannot accommodate the complexity of gender issues.

Three key concepts surface when studying gender issues. These are *difference, salience,* and *negotiation. Difference* refers to the act of viewing gender issues as a unitary theory of male and female contrasts. Thinking about masculine and feminine as binary opposites on a single spectrum of human experience and achievement can lead to a self-fulfilling prophecy. The goal of inquiry and understanding becomes one of documenting and explaining differences, and these distinctions become the standard for viewing the issue. But the complexity of human learning in school settings is much more complex than that. It is a function of gender as well as ethnicity, social class, language, and sexual orientation in a particular setting and time. Thus, bipolar notions of gender have been replaced by patchwork quilts of patterns and colors that represent multiple variables and perspectives.

The second key concept, *salience,* is found in the work of Barrie Thorne (1990), an ethnographer who studies gender as a participant-observer in classrooms, lunchrooms, and playgrounds. Thorne noted that gender separation in a physical sense did not happen all the time, but seemed to be situational. She found that, "The occasions when girls and boys are together are as theoretically and socially significant as when they are apart." Thus, to understand gender relations, ". . . one must grapple with the multiple standpoints, complex and even contradictory meanings, and the varying salience of gender" (pp. 103,111).

86

The last concept is *negotiation*. Students and teachers are participants in a system whereby gender constraints and gender relations are negotiated, sometimes consciously and often unconsciously. The confusing and conflicting array of norms and rules that young females and males encounter in the classroom, lunchroom, playground, and halls necessitates negotiation through *accommodation* and *resistance*. As Jean Anyon (1983) found in her study of fifth graders, girls can resist the middle-class feminine-gender prescriptions by dressing and behaving in ways that teachers find provocative (p. 33). Similarly, boys resist the perceived feminine culture of classrooms by setting up disruptions. Students are active participants in school culture, and they respond collectively and individually to cultural messages. Given the choice of accommodating or resisting a middle-class attitude and behavior toward school and work, many will choose the latter. It seems to help them maintain their independence.

The idea that social structures and values are mainly responsible for the underachievement of groups of students is limiting because it masks the subtleties and complexities of processes that work in schooling. Students are not passive victims in these processes; nor are teachers hapless victims of cultural reproduction systems. Students, teachers, and administrators may contribute to the factors that limit opportunities as well as to those that expand them. Our challenge is to identify crucial structures and processes that will increase life opportunities for all students and maximize the potential of our diversity. Gender is one of four keys.

GENDER BIASES IN SCHOOL

The following paragraphs examine gender biases in important areas of schooling: in testing, content areas, and classroom management.

PSAT and SAT Testing Biases

Every spring approximately one million high school

juniors gather in cafeterias and auditoriums to take the Preliminary Scholastic Aptitude Test/National Merit Qualifying Test (PSAT). Scores from the PSAT, combined with high-school grades, greatly influence the opportunities for college scholarship, and hence, for college education itself.

According to Phyllis Rosser (1989), author of *The SAT Gender Gap: Identifying the Causes*, women are penalized by test biases, resulting in lower overall scores. Rosser also claims, "reliance on biased tests has a severe economic impact on women, who lose millions of dollars in merit scholarship awards . . ." (p.4). In 1987–88 for example, women were eligible for only 36 percent of the 6,000 college scholarships, based on their qualifying score that was 67 points lower than men's. Moreover, opportunities for academic enrichment programs in high schools are also lost as a result of low PSAT scores (Rosser 1989).

The problems with the PSAT and its administration are considerable. First, it inaccurately underestimates academic performance. Grades reported for females in kindergarten through grade 12 are consistently higher than those of their male counterparts; the same holds true during the first year of college. Thus, if women are scoring lower than men on the PSAT but outperforming them academically, the test is persistently, incorrectly predicting women's grades during the first year of college.

In past years of reporting PSAT and Scholastic Aptitude Test (SAT) results, women's verbal scores were higher than men's, and their math scores were lower; in math, the difference during the last 21 years was 41–52 points (Rosser 1989). On SAT scores for 1988, women scored lower in both mean verbal and mathematics sections. These statistics, however, do not reflect grades for the performance of young women and men on other standardized high school tests. (Rosser 1989)

Item analysis of the SAT test revealed persistent effects of bias in the content of the questions. "A larger percentage of women than men chose the correct answers for questions referring to relationships and a larger percentage of men chose the correct answers for questions referring to physical science, sports, and the stock market" (Rosser 1989, p. 7).

The most serious problem with the SAT scores is how some young women interpret them. According to Rosser (1989), young men and women believed that the test was a fair measure of their abilities. That means that young women see themselves as less able than their male contemporaries. For some young women, especially minority women for whom scholarship monies and belief in self are critical, the consequences of this assumption could include opting out of college.

Social Studies

The first consideration in the area of social studies content-bias relates to the previous discussion of standardized tests. The National Assessment of Educational Progress has found that "males consistently outperform females on measures of political knowledge" (Hahn, Bernard-Powers et al. 1985, p.281). State-wide testing of high school juniors in Maine in 1986 resulted in substantially higher scores in social studies for males than females—304–197 (Rosser 1989). In 1985 and 1986, 300,000 eighth-grade students in California were tested under the California Assessment Program (CAP). On the new history/social science test, boys did better on 467 of the questions, while girls scored higher on 253. Whereas, "Boys did better on questions related to war, historical documents (such as the Declaration of Independence, the Constitution, the Bill of Rights), and questions involving geography or chronology . . . . Girls did better on questions related to interpretation of slogans, quotations (except those associated with war), women's rights, or questions in which the focus of the question was a woman (Kneedler 1988). Disparities in scores and performance on specific items suggest that test bias is a problem; moreover, the curriculum knowledge that is being tested is also problematic.

An important point in this issue, both in terms of the SAT and the CAP test, is the collection of data. Lobbies for gender-fair testing have gathered numerous data based on gender and race and/or ethnicity. Now, funding for analysis of this data is a critical need, one that is threatened by budget cutbacks. For example, in California the analysis of performance on the basis of gender has been abandoned due to lack of funding. Data collected and analyzed on the basis of gender, race, ethnicity, and linguistic abilities are key to understanding the dynamics of gender in social studies.

Another vital issue in social studies is *curriculum materials*. Research on social studies instruction in the late seventies found that textbooks dominate social studies instruction (Hahn, Bernard-Powers et al. 1985). This is a particularly important fact because the "most extensively documented inequity in social studies is the underrepresentation and stereotyping of females in social studies textbooks" (p. 281). Despite the virtual revolution in scholarship in ethnic, family, social, and women's histories, textbooks continue to provide inaccurate views of the past and limited role models for young men and young women of all races and ethnic groups. In her 1990 keynote address to the National Council for the Social Studies, Darline Clark-Hine presented evidence that four currently used textbooks consistently failed to provide a significant political and social context for the lives of black women, and that people of color were marginalized. She concluded that the dominant narrative requires a total reconceptualization.

A third gender issue in social studies is *political socialization*. Two studies completed in the mid-seventies reported that young people did not support the idea of women as political leaders (Hahn, Bernard-Powers et al. 1985). A more current study (Gillespie and Spohn, 1987) reported that a substantial percentage of young white and young black men, grades 7–12, did not believe that women were as qualified as men to run the country. A high percentage of the young white women and young black women, 86 percent and 81 percent respectively, thought that women were just as qualified, whereas only 50 percent of white men and 53 percent of black men agreed with the statement. Thus, it is an important dimension of social studies in which males are being undereducated.

Reading

Reading is one of two areas that have been written about extensively in relation to gender. Gender differences favoring girls and young women have been reported in National Assessment of Educational Progress results for almost 20 years, and the differences were sustained in the SATs. However, trends in both the NAEP and the SAT tests indicate that the gender gap is closing. In fact, nationally, men outscored women on the 1987 SAT by approximately 10 points (Rosser 1989).

Potentially more critical than the closing gender gap in reading and verbal skills is the low performance of minority youths on standardized reading tests, something that may or may not be salient to gender. Forty-five percent of white 17-year-olds are "adept" in reading according to the NAEP 1984 test results, which means they can find, summarize, and analyze complicated information (NAEP 1985). In contrast, only 16 to 20 percent of Black and Hispanic 17-year-olds are adept readers. Drop-out rates for Black and Hispanic males are reported to be generally higher than for females of all races and ethnic groups, and this may be related to reading and the extent to which the needs of this population are not being met. Data collection and analysis that combines gender, ethnicity, and linguistic abilities can illuminate these potentially salient issues.

Math, Science, and Computer Education

Although science educators are currently concerned about national levels of achievement, the participation and achievement of women of color, of women in general, and of minorities in general have been particular concerns since the

91

early seventies. Nevertheless, women and minority students are underrepresented in higher education mathematics and science departments and in technical fields. According to NAEP findings, "More than half of the nation's 17-year-olds appear to be inadequately prepared either to perform competently jobs that require technical skills or to benefit from specialized on-the-job training.... At age 17 ... only one-third of the females demonstrated the ability to analyze scientific material and data," and for Blacks and Hispanics, the proportion was even lower (NAEP 1985, pp. 30–31). Research on motivation has found that the male/female differences in achievement cannot be explained entirely by attitudes toward the subject, however. There are other circumstances and variables affecting performance (Steinkamp and Maehr 1984).

One of the most significant recent findings indicates that gender differences among high school students are declining, and that when science processes are separated from knowledge, differences only occur in measures of knowledge. This attests to the fluidity of gendered learning and refutes notions of immutable sex differences. Research on mathematics achievement has found that girls' and boys' achievement is relatively equal up until ages 12–13, when males seem to develop an advantage (Hyde, Fennema, and Lamon 1990). This advantage increases up through high school and into college years, when females and minorities self-select out of fields that have advanced mathematics prerequisites. SAT scores for mathematical ability have favored males for about 20 years; however, researchers have found these differences to be disappearing (Linn and Hyde 1989).

Computer education is recognized as a significant area of competency for students in the late twentieth and early twenty-first centuries. The potential of computer education for reorganizing educational settings makes computer competency especially important. Thus, findings on computer use are particularly compelling. Peg Griffin and Michael Cole (1987) wrote that computer use is making "... the position of minorities and women, relatively worse with respect to Anglo/ male norms used in such comparisons." They reported that:

1. More computers are being placed in the hands of middle- and upper-class children.
2. When computers are placed in the hands of poor children, they are used for rote drill and practice instead of for the "cognitive enrichment" that they provide middle- and upper-class students.
3. Female students have less involvement than male students with computers in schools, irrespective of race or ethnicity.

These findings in performance differences for males and females in math, science, and computers suggest the need for change in several areas. Teacher training needs to include information about contexts that foster equal participation for males, females, and minorities in all three of these areas. Continued support for elementary science teachers who find time and resources at a premium is critical. Interdisciplinary teaching that incorporates teaching reading with science and social studies will increase the number of minutes that young women and minorities are provided in instruction. After-school programs and special programs, such as the *Equals* project at the Lawrence Hall of Science in Berkeley, California, can provide out-of-school time for working in hands-on science, mathematics, and computing, thereby developing confidence in abilities and increasing interest in careers (Skolnick, Langbon, and Day 1982). Increased requirements at the secondary level; increased support for young women and minorities in one-to-one and small-group work and peer tutoring; and counseling that is sensitive to race, class, and ethnic issues may help students to accurately estimate their abilities and value their own knowledge and understanding.

Classroom Organization and Instruction

The final topic for consideration in the discussion of gender and achievement is *classroom organization* and *instruction*. Group work based on theory guiding practice holds great promise for maximizing learning and harnessing the effects of gender, ethnicity, and race on classroom achievement. By providing training for group roles, very specific feedback on demonstrated student strengths, and modeling for equal treatment of humans, we can increase learning in math and science, group problem-solving, and prosocial behavior for minorities and young women. The program for Complex Instruction at Stanford University in California, is an example of a program that trains educators to use instruction that is designed to be gender friendly as well as racially, ethnically, and linguistically friendly (Cohen 1988).

Considering the importance of context holds the promise of improving instruction for everyone. *Context,* in this case, means the context for learning. Providing meaningful and challenging problems (or contexts) that house various cognitive learning tasks is more effective than direct instruction or seatwork. Researchers have found that the principles that influence learning in early childhood are very useful for older children and adults. Rather than isolating instruction into discrete bounded tasks, instruction and learning for the next century needs to be placed in a context that includes problems similar to those that students will encounter in their life journey. We need to increase the cognitive complexity and build on the strengths and challenges that our diverse populations have brought us.

CONCLUSION

Our work in sex equity in the sixties and seventies raised questions and built a scaffolding from which we continue to profit. The problem of equal access to opportunities and education for young women of all races and ethnic groups has not been totally redressed, but we now know that it will not go away or slide into oblivion.

In the eighties and nineties, research and scholarship in the content areas as well as in pedagogy, classroom management, achievement motivation, and testing has led us to an appreciable understanding of the complexity of gendered systems. Gender is an omnipresent reality that rarely stands alone. An appreciation of salience, context, negotiation, and a healthy skepticism of any easy prescription for progress will carry us into the next century. In education, it is our diverse and gendered student population who provide the motivation and the modeling for us to move into the twenty-first century.

REFERENCES

Anyon, J. 1983. Intersections of gender and class: Accommodation and resistance by working-class and affluent females to contradictory sex-role ideologies. In *Gender, class, and education*, edited by S.Walker and L. Barton, 33. Sussex: Falmer Press.

Clark-Hine, D. 1990. The treatment of minorities in U.S. history textbooks. Oral address to the National Council for the Social Studies, November 1990. Anaheim, Ca.

Cohen, E. 1988. *Designing groupwork: Strategies for the heterogenous classroom.* New York: Teachers College Press.

Cole, M. and Griffin, P. eds. 1987. *Contextual factors in education.* Madison: Wisconsin Center for Education Research.

Farmer, H. and Seliger-Sidney, J. 1985. Sex equity in career and vocational education. In *Handbook for achieving sex equity in education*, edited by S. Klein. Baltimore, Md.: John Hopkins University Press.

Gillespie, D. and Spohn, C. 1987. Adolescents' attitudes toward women in politics: The effect of gender and race. *Gender and Society* 1 (2): 208-18.

Grant, C. and Sleeter, C. 1986. *After the school bell rings.* Philadelphia: Falmer Press.

Hahn, C.; Bernard-Powers, J.; . 1985. Sex equity in the social studies. In *Handbook for achieving sex equity in education*, edited by S. Klein, 281. Baltimore, Md.: John Hopkins University Press.

Kneedler, P. 1988. Differences between boys and girls on California's new statewide assessments in history-social science. Paper presented at the California Council for the Social Studies, March 1988.

Linn, M.C. and Shibley-Hyde, J. 1989. Gender, mathematics, and science. *Educational Researcher* 18 (8): 22.

National Assessment of Educational Progress. 1985. *The reading report card.* Princeton, N.J.: Educational Testing Service.

National Assessment of Educational Progress. 1988. *The science report card.* Princeton, N.J.: Educational Testing Service.

Rosser, P. 1989. *The SAT gender gap: Identifying the causes.* Washington, DC: Center for Women Policy Studies.

Shibley-Hyde, J.; Fennema, E.; and Lamon, S.L. 1990. Gender differences in mathematics performance: A meta-analysis. *Psychological Bulletin* 107 (2): 139. Skolnick, J.; Langbort, C.; and Day, L. 1982. *How to encourage girls in math and science.* Englewood Cliffs, N.J.: Prentice Hall.

Steinkamp, M.W. and Maehr, M.L. 1984. Gender differences in motivational orientations toward achievement in school science: A quantitative synthesis. *American Education Research Journal* 21 (1): 43.

Thorne, B. 1990. Children and gender. In *Theoretical perspectives on sexual difference*, edited by D. Rhode, 103 & 111. New Haven, Ct.: Yale University Press.

Chapter 7

EVALUATION PRACTICES FOR THE MULTICULTURAL CLASSROOM

by Ronald J. Samuda and John Lewis

The United States, like Canada, Australia, Britain, and certain Western European countries, has become a *de facto* multicultural society. Whether the principle of multiculturalism as an official tenet of government exists or not is not the issue. What is important is the existence of a drastically changed demographic reality with serious consequences for the public schools.

Teachers are now faced with the problems of accommodating a multicultural and ethnically heterogeneous population of students in the schools. If the ideal is to maximize the principle of equality of educational opportunity, then traditional evaluation and placement procedures biased in favor of the middle-class WASP mainstream must be replaced by a more equitable system.

In addressing the issue of the changing population of students, it is also important to recognize that traditional teacher training has provided many practicing teachers with a fixed belief in the rightness of standardized norm-referenced assessment techniques. There are even some educators who still cling to the notion that all children should be assessed by the standard objective instruments and that students should be grouped according to their demonstrated ability to perform in the traditional curriculum and teaching/learning programs. Indeed, there are renowned educators and psychologists who championed the sorting process of IQ testing and interpreted the lower scores of some ethnic and cultural minorities as due to inherent and racially determined factors. It was precisely that kind of thinking that led Lewis Terman, originator of the Stanford-Binet test and one of the most eminent psychologists of the day, to make the following comments when confronted with the test performance of a pair of Mexican-American and Indian children:

> Their dullness seems to be racial, or at least inherent in the family stocks from which they come...there will be discovered enormous significant racial differences which cannot be wiped out by any scheme of mental culture. Children of this group should be segregated in special classes .... There is no possibility of convincing society that they should not be allowed to reproduce. (Kamin 1976, pp. 374–382)

That quotation epitomizes the three aspects of racism involved in interpreting minority-student test results—*structural, technical,* and *scientific. Structural racism* could be more blandly described as ethnocentrism or a collective mind set that requires each individual be judged according to the same standards, procedures, and values, regardless of cultural or class differences. *Technical racism* refers to the use of correlations and the citations of concurrent and predictive validity as statistical evidence to justify the labeling of minorities and the placement consequences of test results. *Scientific racism* implies a belief in the racial inheritance of inferior mental stock by those who are not of Northwestern European lineage.

The struggles toward the civil rights of minorities, initiated in the sixties, intensified in the decade of the seventies and affected the assessment and placement of students in the schools, as in the case of *Larry P. v. Wilson Riles,* where a California student was misplaced in a school for the mentally retarded because of an IQ score. The exposure of discrimination in the use and interpretation of standardized tests, and the enlightenment that followed in the eighties, have largely dispelled the notions of the superiority of students who derive from Northwestern European heritage while denigrating students from Africa, Native America, or other non-European stock.

More and more, the available empirical evidence has demonstrated that mental capacity and learning potential are equally distributed across all races, ethnic groups, and social classes. Accordingly, equality of educational opportunity should result in equality of educational outcome. There are, therefore, no empirical grounds to support the overrepresentation of some minorities in special education, vocational, or basic level programs; or the underrepresentation of minority students in gifted/enriched programs.

The primary concern is not with the race or ethnic background or socioeconomic circumstances of students, but with their home and those environmental factors affecting the developmental pattern of the individual. In other words, there are ethnic-minority students who are perfectly equipped to be tested by traditional IQ tests. The results will validly predict achievement because of their middle-class orientation. The key issue is whether or not experience derived from the home and the social and linguistic environment match the kinds of items and processes involved in the tests. Traditional tests will not be valid for students who are culturally different even though there might seem to be a match between low aptitude scores and achievement.

Many ethnic minority students are often assessed and labeled incorrectly by tests designed by middle-class psychologists for middle-class children. Those students who veer from the mainstream achieve poorly because the programs of instruction do not match their learning needs. Furthermore, traditional standardized tests—especially when used with clinical and objective protocol—cannot reveal much about the atypical student. The problem is more than academic, for the cultural environment affects such characteristics as motivation, anxiety, interpersonal relationships, speed, and familiarity with objective methods of testing. The following is therefore intended to summarize alternative ways to obtain information to help teachers improve the learning situation in the schools.

INNOVATIVE APPROACHES IN ASSESSMENT

Factor analytic studies have been useful in identifying the number of specific aptitudes that make up overall mental ability, but they fall short in explaining how a specific ability or cluster of abilities develops. Mental tests would be more useful if, in addition to measuring intelligence as a product, they also could identify the process—the means by which intelligence changes as an individual acquires new experiences. James Cattell's theory of *fluid* and *crystallized intelligence* represents a departure from the two-factor theory.

According to Cattell, *fluid intelligence* refers to a basic capacity to adapt to new situations. It is also an inherent capacity for learning and problem solving that is independent of both education and cultural influences. In order to adapt to novel situations, fluid intelligence must encompass flexible inductive skills.

Crystallized intelligence emerges from a person's use of fluid intelligence to interact with society. It is therefore a product of formal education. The way crystallized intelligence organizes knowledge and concepts reflects how the member of a given society processes information and solves problems. Because these abilities are already developed, they can be quantified and assembled to make up tests for general mental ability. The outcome of such measures is necessarily static in nature.

Intelligence in Cattell's conception, then, develops from an active mind that is malleable and responsive to instruction. Intelligence not only processes information, but also anticipates new situations and plans effective solutions. It follows that any adequate assessment of intelligence as described by Cattell must address both these fluid and crystallized characteristics.

With this view of intelligence in mind, psychologists have set out to devise new approaches to intellectual assessment that take into account not only static knowledge but also cognitive processes. While these approaches still depend on the use of tests and test scores as a measure of mental ability, they also incorporate teaching and clinical observation to determine the individual cognitive style and possible learning deficits of any one student. Such assessment, therefore, is an ongoing process in which the teacher monitors and reinforces academic progress and cognitive development. Many studies have advocated the need to shift from conventional methods of assessing minority students to these new approaches (Salvia and Ysseldyke 1978). Two of the most vital approaches are: *comprehensive individual assessment* and *dynamic assessment.*

Comprehensive Individual Assessment

The goal of *comprehensive individual assessment* is to enhance accuracy in evaluating the current level and mode of intellectual functioning of a student within the context of his or her cultural and experiential background. Specific learning needs are diagnosed and assets are identified to help the teacher formulate a personalized remedial program. In practice, such an assessment process involves a team consisting of a counselor or psychometrician, a teacher, and a school administrator. Often, parents participate as well. The team gathers student data for the assessment through testing, observation, consultation, and diagnosis. The assessment follows these guidelines:

- Diagnostic decisions, placement, and program changes in any counseling situation should be based on a wide range of information about the student.
- Assessment should result from a team deliberation on such information as how the student's performance is influenced by acculturation, language skills, behavior mode, socioeconomic background, and ethnocultural identity.
- The appraisal of the student's needs, strengths, weaknesses, and level of present cognitive functioning should be made with reference to the background data outlined in the previous guideline.
- The main assessment objective should be to define and

101

design a teaching or remedial program that would best help the student profit from the school system.

- The remedial program should be carried out and monitored regularly by the assessment team.

In contrast to a single score, as obtained from a conventional IQ test, the comprehensive profile is made up of information from a wide range of data sources, namely: observational data, school records and other available documents, language dominance, educational assessment, sensorimotor and/or developmental data, adaptive behavior data, medical records, and personality assessment (including self-report). Intellectual assessment should be performed last, so that its result can be interpreted in the context of all the other information gathered.

Comprehensive assessment is a continuous process. As individuals develop, their intellectual and achievement profiles change. Identifying a student's information-processing modes and other relevant factors for each subject area would help teachers design appropriate learning materials and procedures to meet that individual's needs. The emphasis should be on helping students maximize competencies and opportunities, particularly in the case of minorities (Reschley 1981, pp. 1094–102).

With this in mind, Harold Dent (1976) has suggested that assessment procedures should follow four directives. First, the assessment must provide an accurate appraisal of a student's current level and mode of functioning within the context of his or her cultural background and experience. Second, it must identify specific educational needs rather than focus on perceived or inferred intellectual deficits. Third, it must focus on learning assets and strengths as the basis for the development of new learning skills. Finally, it must be a dynamic, ongoing process.

Dynamic Assessment

Unlike leaders in psychometric tradition who treat

intelligence as a static product, L.S. Vygotsky (1978) perceives intelligence as a dynamic process that changes with development and learning. As a learner interacts with other people, his or her learning stimulates cognitive development. As cognitive development proceeds, "zone of proximal development" can be delineated to reflect the gap between the learner's actual development and his or her development potential. This potential enables the psychologist or teacher to help improve the learner's mental ability. In this sense, assessment is dynamic and helpful. Vygotsky defines the *zone of proximal development* as:

> The distance between the actual development level as determined by independent problem solving and the level of potential development as determined through problem solving under adult guidance or in collaboration with more capable peers. (p. 86)

The size of this zone is determined by adapting conventional IQ tests within a "test-teach-test" format. An individual is first given a test (or part of it) to determine which items he or she can perform correctly and which present difficulty. After this initial performance, the psychologist or teacher provides help in completing the difficult items by appropriate prompting until competence is achieved. Finally, similar test items are administered again to ascertain the degree to which learning has helped the student to perform better.

Several methods can be used to make comprehensive and dynamic assessments. These include the Budoff, Feuerstein, and Kaufman methods.

THE BUDOFF METHOD

Milton Budoff's method of assessment (1974) begins with testing the individual in a series of both familiar and novel tasks. The results provide a baseline measure that can be compared to subsequent performance. This is the diagnostic phase. The second phase involves a teaching and learning process, in which the tester (the teacher) explains to the testee (the student) the principles of thought and logic required to perform the previous tasks. Teachers can impart either general reasoning skills or basic concepts. Then tasks in the original test are rearranged from easy to difficult, and the testee is asked to do them again, beginning with the easiest item and proceeding to progressively more difficult ones. This methodology enables the assessment of two dimensions of the effectiveness of the teaching: the existence of student's improvement and the degree of improvement. From these clinical observations, the data can be acquired on both the learning potential of the testee and the manner and speed with which performance is being improved. The student's preferred cognitive modality can also be identified; that is, whether auditory or kinesthetic inputs are most helpful in attaining an improved understanding.

The above method of assessment can be used for a single task or a number of tasks. In the case of several tasks, a battery of tests is employed. So far, Budoff's research has concentrated on assessment that uses a single-task approach. He also believes in the use of nonverbal tests, such as the Kohs Block Designs Test (Sattler 1982) and the Raven's Colored Progressive Matrices (Raven 1965) for assessing and improving children's reasoning abilities. Because both the test items and the training exercises are free of cultural bias, children of diverse backgrounds can gain true cognitive experience unhampered by negative situational factors, such as the effects of failure in school, cultural block, and language deficiencies. This approach has been proven effective in improving children's cognitive ability scores (Budoff 1974).

THE FEUERSTEIN METHOD

Reuven Feuerstein's major concern (Feuerstein and Hoffman 1982) has been to assess the untapped cognitive potential of individuals, particularly the culturally deprived, and to remedy any deficiencies through an active intervention process that helps the individual build a new and effective cognitive structure. He believes that the acquisition of such a structure enables a person of low mental ability to become more adaptable, flexible, and therefore generally more capable of comprehending, planning, and solving problems.

A clear distinction is made between cultural deprivation and cultural difference in Feuerstein's scheme of thinking. The *culturally-different individual* is simply one who is a member of a minority group within a society dominated by a mainstream culture that is different. Because of this background, the individual may suffer from not being tuned into what is going on in society and/or from a lack of economic opportunities. But such deficiencies may change as the individual acquires the essential skills of achieving success within the social structure. In any case, a strong affiliation with his or her own minority culture can often provide the culturally-different individual with a sound psychological foundation to deal effectively with the requirements and expectations of the dominant culture.

A *culturally-deprived individual*, on the other hand, is a person who is deprived of his or her own background culture—one who has, in effect, become alienated from any cultural affiliation. This alienation may be caused by any number of single or interactive factors: social class, physical factors, religion, psychological factors, and/or learning. Whatever the cause, cultural deprivation often leads to poor cognitive ability, which reduces the individual's chances of keeping up with peers and the school's expectations. Even manifestations, such as a lack of motivation and the ability to learn and change in therapeutic and remedial situations, can signal cultural deprivation. It is not difficult to realize that, under these circumstances, the use of conventional IQ tests for assessment would only compound an already unfavorable situation if it indicated that an individual has a low IQ score. A different approach of assessment is needed if change is intended to be a logical follow-up of that assessment.

In their investigation into the problems confronting the culturally deprived, Feuerstein and Mildred Hoffman (1982) conclude that such individuals suffer from "a disruption of intergenerational transmission and mediational process." Not only are they deprived of the learning experiences mediated by parents that normally should occur during childhood, but they also are prevented from developing a sense of order about the environment and from formulating effective cognitive schemes with which to handle daily life problems.

In normal childhood, interactions between child and parents are typically replete with examples of mediated learning. In this process, the parents selectively accept or reject certain stimuli to present to the child; in effect, they filter, frame, schedule, and sequence events, and mediate relationships of time, space, causality, and affection. Through these experiences, children gradually construct their cognitive structures and link themselves with their cultural past and social reality.

Every culture provides a structure within which the organization, interpretation, and understanding of events and relationships can occur through exposure and experience. It is this organization of experience that links individuals to their society. It also enables them to be flexible, adaptable, and creative in rooting themselves with the past, handling the present, and anticipating the future in the context of their cultural milieu. Language plays an important part in this process, as do other forms of communication and sharing. Feuerstein suggests that a mediated learning experience (M.L.E.), such as one that occurs between children and parents in the normal process of development, is necessary to initiate every member of a society into the universal cognitive structure of that society. For those who have been deprived of this initiation, Feuerstein believes that the introduction of M.L.E. intended to fill in the gaps left by deprivation is helpful.

If we assume that a culturally-deprived person, whether a child or adult, has a much higher potential than he or she has been able to demonstrate in conventional IQ tests, then a teacher, acting as a mediator, can help improve this person's cognitive ability by providing alternative perceptions and interpretations of the world. In order to do so, the teacher must

106

first gain an understanding of both the individual's intelligence and cognitive potential.

The Learning Potential Assessment Device

Feuerstein uses a dynamic assessment approach that he calls the Learning Potential Assessment Device (L.P.A.D.). He begins with a clear delineation of psychometric goals, namely: (1) to assess the student's cognitive modifiability by observing the student functioning in situations designed to produce change, (2) to assess the extent of modifiability in terms of cognitive functioning, and how significant a student's attained functioning is in the hierarchy of universal cognitive operations ranging from perception to abstract thinking, (3) to determine the transfer value of what is learned in one area to other areas of operation, and (4) to identify the student's preferred modalities for learning and the problem-solving strategies that work best.

According to the study of cross-cultural assessment by Norman Sundberg and Linda Gonzalez (1981), the Feuerstein L.P.A.D. approach contributes significantly toward clarifying the special needs of minority individuals and groups. Examples of L.P.A.D. item types include the organization of dots, the representational stencil design, complex figures, the plateaux, functional associative recall, and John Raven's matrices and set variations.

The assessment process engages both the student and the assessor or counselor in active modification operations. As the client performs the given tasks, the counselor intervenes whenever necessary to present alternative ways of perceiving, interpreting, and problem solving. Any change is noted as well as the amount of intervention required to produce the change. On the basis of these observations, the counselor then predicts the level of change potential.

The use of the L.P.A.D. focuses on the *process* rather than on the *product*. The instrument can help to tap acquisition components and performance components of intelligence as well as to identify where deficits lie. Deficits may lie at the *input level*, indicating such behaviors as impulsivity and blurred perception; at the *elaboration level*, demonstrated by difficulties in defining a problem and impaired planning behavior; or at the *output level*, evidenced by egocentric communication and impulsive acting-out.

Deficits in the three levels of operation are fluidly interactive and must be considered as a whole. In terms of the need for mediation, the research of Harvey Narrol (Narrol, Silverman, and Waksman 1982) shows that an individual is amenable to remedial help if he or she exhibits deficits at either the input or output phase. In contrast, elaboration deficits may reflect a limited ceiling in cognitive capacity, which would mean that there is not a great deal of room for cognitive reconstruction.

When viewed as a special assessment method aimed at facilitating therapeutic measures, the L.P.A.D. serves to meet the needs of people who are culturally deprived. Administered properly, tests using the dynamic assessment approach can inform us of the individual's capacity to grasp an underlying principle and of the amount of work required to teach a principle. It can also shed some light on what is learned to solve new problems, the individual's modality preference in cognitive operations, and the effects of mediation strategies on changing cognitive structures.

THE KAUFMAN METHOD

Alan Kaufman (Kaufman and Kaufman 1982) is concerned with the assessment of fluid intelligence and achievement. The Kaufman Assessment Battery for Children also called the K-ABC, measures intellectual functioning in two broad categories: mental composite processing and achievement. Mental composite processing and simultaneous processing are assessed through close observation, as the tests are administered individually.

The K-ABC is made up of 16 subtests designed to measure different elements of children's intellectual capacity. Ten of these are used to assess intellectual functioning, while the remaining six assess achievement. The battery is standardized on a nationwide sample of normal and exceptional students between 2.5 and 12.5 years of age. The tests are administered individually and involve only rudimentary verbal skills. In fact, a nonverbal scale is included to test children who have language differences or language disorders. Norms have been established to reflect sociocultural factors, which make the tests useful for assessing those from ethnic-minority backgrounds.

CONCLUSION

Based on preliminary research results, it seems that both the L.P.A.D. and the K-ABC are more appropriate assessment devices for testing minority children than the WISC-R and SOMPA. Both methods minimize factual information and general learned content; they concentrate on problem-solving tasks of a nonverbal and culture-fair nature. Both incorporate a training component to help the testee who does not understand the tasks involved. The Feuerstein approach trains the testee in order to measure learning potential, while the Kaufman method does the same thing so that more reliable scores can be obtained.

As a whole, the innovative approaches to mental-ability assessment have shifted the focus away from quantitative product scores to qualitative observations and interpretations of the process of mental-ability functioning. This "dynamic assessment" is based on the assumption that intelligence is a multifaceted, multidimensional, and fluid construct that continually undergoes change (Samuda et al. 1991). This approach attempts to determine not only the characteristics of the various components of intelligence, but also how they function. One way of doing this is to use the verbalizations of testees as a vehicle to tap their underlying cognitive processes as they work through various problems.

We have come a long way since the kind of labeling and placement that occurred until well into the seventies. Fortunately, it is unlikely that in today's San Francisco school system, Larry P. would suffer the fate of placement in a class for the mentally retarded. We have discovered the means to find the truth. But that was only one part of the task. What we have not done sufficiently so far is to communicate that truth to the educators who make decisions affecting the lives of minority students. The truths that we have discovered have not yet reached many of the faculties of education and social science. Although some teachers still cling to redundant and ineffective practices in assessing their culturally-different students, enlightened educators, psychologists, and counselors are moving to a new perspective by using much of what has been described in this chapter.

REFERENCES

Budoff, M. 1974. *Learning potential and educability among the educable mentally retarded (rep. no. 312312).* Cambridge, Mass.: Research Institute for Educational Problems, Cambridge Mental Health Association.

Dent, H. 1976. Assessing black children for mainstream placement. In *Mainstreaming and the minority child,* edited by R. Jones and F. Wilderson. Minneapolis, Minn.: CEC Publications.

Feuerstein, R. and Hoffman, M.B. 1982. Intergenerational conflict of rights: Cultural imposition and self-realization. Unpublished manuscript.

Kamin, L. 1976. Heritability, intelligence, politics, and psychology: II. In *The IQ controversy,* edited by N.J. Block and G. Dworkin, 374–82. New York: Pantheon Books.

Kaufman, A.S. and Kaufman, N.L. 1982. *Kaufman assessment battery for children: Interpretative manual.* Circle Pines, Minn.: American Guidance Service.

Narrol, H.; Silverman, H.; and Waksman, M. 1982. Developing cognitive potential in vocational high school students. *Journal of Educational Research* 76: 106–12.

Raven, J.C. 1965. *Guide to using the colored matrices sets A AB B.* London: H.K. Lewis.

Reschley, D.J. 1981. Psychological testing in educational classification and placement. *American Psychologist* 36: 1094–102.

Salvia, J. and Ysseldyke, R. B. 1978. *Assessment in special and remedial education.* Boston: Houghton-Mifflin.

Samuda, R.J. et al. 1991. *Assessment and placement of minority students.* Toronto: Hogrefe/ISSP.

Sattler, J.M. 1982. *Assessment of children's intelligence and special abilities.* 2nd ed. Boston: Allyn and Bacon.

Sundberg, N. and Gonzalez, L. 1981. Cross-cultural and cross-ethnic assessment overview and issues. In *Advances in psychological assessment,* Vol. 5, edited by P. McReynolds. San Francisco: Jossey-Bass.

Vygotsky, L.S. 1978. *Mind in society: The development of higher psychological processes.* Cambridge, Mass.: Harvard University Press.

Chapter 8

WE SPEAK IN MANY TONGUES: LANGUAGE DIVERSITY AND MULTICULTURAL EDUCATION

by Sonia Nieto

The United States is becoming a truly multilingual nation, if not in policy, at least in practice. While the battle by the conservative right to make English the sole and official language of the country rages on, our classrooms, communities, and workplaces are becoming more linguistically diverse (National Education Association 1988; Daniel 1990). The increase in the number of students who speak a native language other than English has become dramatic, and this trend is expected to continue. The number of immigrants to the United States during the 1970s and 1980s was among the largest in history. Legal immigration alone between 1980 and 1990 was almost nine million, equaling that of the peak immigration decade of 1900–1910. About one-third of this immigration has been from Asia and another third from Latin America. In addition, it is estimated that the number of students who speak a language other than English will increase from just over two million in 1986 to more than five million by 2020. Another indication of the enormous changes taking place in our society is the prediction that by the year 2050 the Latino population will have tripled in number and the Asian population will have increased tenfold (Kellogg 1988; Muller and Espenshade 1985; National Coalition of Advocates for Students 1988; Natriello, McDill, and Pallas 1990; Feistristzer 1986).

These statistics are cause for concern for the many teachers who must grapple with the dilemmas posed by the linguistic and educational differences that students bring to our schools. The purpose of this chapter is to explore the growing linguistic diversity in our society and schools in order to propose a different and more productive way of approaching the educational challenges they bring. Rather than continuing to view linguistic diversity as a problem to be corrected, we must change our thinking and consider it an asset for our classrooms and for society in general. For that reason, research focusing on the importance of native-language development in school achievement will be considered carefully. Based on the research reviewed and on a reconceptualization of language diversity within schools, I then will propose several implications for school policies and practices.

LANGUAGE DIVERSITY AND MULTICULTURAL EDUCATION: EXPANDING THE FRAMEWORK

To understand language issues in a more comprehensive way, we need to expand the framework with which we view linguistic diversity. There are several ways in which to do this. These include:

- perceiving language diversity as a positive rather than as a negative condition,
- developing an awareness of the key role that language discrimination has played in U.S. educational history,
- removing the compensatory status of programs for linguistically diverse students,
- understanding the crucial role of bilingual education within a multicultural perspective, and
- redefining the benefits of linguistic diversity for all students.

Viewing Bilingualism as an Asset

In the United States, we have generally been socialized to think of language diversity as a negative rather than as a positive condition. Yet in most other countries in the world, bilingualism and multilingualism are the order of the day. The prestige accorded to language diversity is a highly complex issue that

113

depends upon the region of the country one resides in, the country itself, the language variety spoken there, where and when one has learned to speak specific languages, and of course, the ethnicity and class of the speaker. Sometimes bilingualism is highly regarded. This is usually the case with those who are well educated and have a high standing within their society. At other times, bilingualism is seen as a sign of low status. This is usually the case with those who are poor and powerless within their society, even if they happen to speak a multitude of languages (Giles, Scherer, and Taylor 1979; Phillipson 1988). It is evident that issues of *status* and *power* must be taken into account in reconceptualizing language diversity. This means developing an awareness that racism and ethnocentrism are at the core of policies and practices that limit the use of languages other than the officially recognized high-status language in schools and in the society in general. That is, when particular languages are prohibited or denigrated, the voices of those who speak them are silenced and rejected as well.

English is the language of power in the United States. For those who speak it as a native language, monolingualism is an asset. In our society, bilingualism is usually considered an asset only for those who are dominant in English but have learned another language as a second language. On the other hand, those who speak a language associated with low prestige and limited power as their native tongue are often regarded as deficient. Speaking with a Parisian French accent, for example, may be regarded as a mark of high status in some parts of the country, while speaking Canadian French or Haitian Creole usually is not. Likewise, speaking Castilian Spanish tends to be regarded more positively than speaking Latin American or Caribbean Spanish, which are often viewed within the general population as inferior varieties of the language.

For some groups, then, bilingualism is seen as a handicap. This is usually the case with our Latino, American Indian, Asian, and other Caribbean students, those who represent the majority of the language-minority students in our classrooms. Linguistically, there is nothing wrong with the languages they speak. That is, for purposes of communication, these languages are as valid as any others. However, socially and politically, they are accorded low status. Students who speak these languages are perceived as having a "problem," and the problem is defined as fluency in a language other than English. Because society in general, and schools in particular, define this as a problem, the purpose of education becomes the elimination of all signs of the native language. This is often done by well-meaning educators who perceive their students' fluency in another language as a handicap to their learning English and climbing the social ladder (Hurtado and Rodriguez 1989).

Developing an Awareness of Linguicism

United States educational history is replete with examples of language discrimination or what Tove Skutnabb-Kangas (1988) has called *linguicism*. Specifically, she defines linguicism as "ideologies and structures that are used to legitimate, effectuate, and reproduce an unequal division of power and resources (both material and nonmaterial) between groups that are defined on the basis of language" (p. 13). Entire communities, starting with American Indian nations and enslaved African Americans, have been denied the use of their native languages for either communication or education. This is evident in policies that forbid the use of other languages in schools as well as in the lack of equal educational opportunity for youngsters who cannot understand the language of instruction (Weinberg 1977; Cummins 1989; *Lau v. Nichols*). While this is particularly evident within racially and economically oppressed groups, linguicism has not been limited to these but has in fact been a widespread policy with *all* languages other than English in our society. The massive obliteration of the German language is a case in point. While German was almost on a par with English as a language of communication during the eighteenth and nineteenth centuries, and was in fact one of the most common languages used in bilingual programs during parts of our history, it was exterminated by xenophobic policies immediately prior to and after World War I (Castellanos 1983; Keller and van Hooft 1982).

Because of the tremendous pressures faced by those who spoke languages other than English, the fact that giving up one's language is a terrible and unnecessary sacrifice was often not recognized. Even today, it is still common to hear of children punished for speaking their native language, or of notes sent home to parents who barely speak English that ask them not to speak their native language with their children. While nowadays there is more of an awareness of the extreme ethnocentrism of such practices, the fact that they continue to exist is an indication of our ingrained reluctance to perceive language diversity in positive terms. In developing a more positive framework for linguistic diversity, it is absolutely crucial that we learn how language discrimination has been used to discredit and disenfranchise those who speak languages other than English.

Removing the Compensatory Label From Linguistic Diversity

Generally speaking, approaches geared toward students who speak a language other than English are compensatory in nature. That is, they respond to language diversity as if it were an illness to be cured. Thus, most approaches emphasize using the native language only as a bridge to English. When English is learned sufficiently well, the reasoning goes, the bridge can be burned and the student is well on his or her way to achieving academic success.

There are several problems with this reasoning. First, a compensatory approach assumes only that students are *lacking* in something, rather than that they also possess certain skills and talents. Instead of perceiving fluency in another language as an asset to be cherished, it is seen as something that needs repair. Using the students' literacy in their native language as a basis for the development of literacy in their second language is not

116

usually considered a viable option. Thus, students are expected to start all over again. Not only do they flounder in English, but they often forget their native language in the process. In addition, even when language-minority students are in bilingual programs, they are frequently removed too quickly and often end up in special education classes (Cummins 1984). Most of the approaches used to help language minority students in school are based on this compensatory framework (Ovando and Collier 1985). Yet research in this area has suggested that, in general, students need between five and seven years to make a successful transition from their native language to English (Cummins 1981; Collier 1989a). Ironically, when they fail to achieve, the blame is often placed on bilingual programs, rather than on premature departure from bilingual programs. Schools need to turn around preconceived notions of language diversity that may lead to policies and practices that jeopardize the very students whom we are trying to reach.

In order to expand our framework for linguistic diversity, then, we need to develop practices that build on students' language skills rather than tear them down. Programs such as *maintenance* or *developmental bilingual education*, in which students are encouraged to develop literacy and continue using both English and their native language, represent a very different approach to language diversity. In programs such as these, students' native language is not considered a crutch to lean on until they master the real language of schooling. Rather, their native language is recognized as valid, not only while they learn English, but also in the acquisition of knowledge in general. *Two-way bilingual programs*, where both language-minority students and monolingual speakers of English are integrated, afford another way of validating both languages of instruction. In addition, students in these programs learn to appreciate the language and culture of others, and to empathize with their peers in the difficult process of developing fluency in a language not their own. Such programs have also been found to be successful in promoting academic achievement (Collier 1989b).

117

Understanding the Role of Linguistic Diversity Within Multicultural Education

In expanding the framework for language diversity, we also need to redefine it within the field of multicultural education. One of the primary goals of multicultural education is to build on the strengths that students bring to school. Unfortunately, even within multicultural education, the benefits of language diversity are rarely considered. The most enlightened and inclusive frameworks for multicultural education fail to take into account the significance of language differences. Although race, class, and gender are often considered integral to multicultural education, language, which does not fit neatly into any of these categories, is not (Sleeter and Grant 1988). While it is true that most language-minority students within United States schools are also from racially and economically oppressed communities, language differences cannot be relegated to either racial or class distinctions alone. Language diversity in and of itself needs to be considered as an important difference through which we can better understand both the talents and the needs that students bring to school.

The failure of many proponents of multicultural education to seriously consider linguistic diversity or of supporters of bilingual education to understand the goals of multicultural education leads to a curious schism: In one corner, we have multicultural education, while in the other we have bilingual education. This artificial separation often results in the perception that multicultural education is for African American and other students of color who speak English, while bilingual education is only for Latino and other students who speak a language other than English as their native language. This perception is reinforced by the fact that each of these fields has its own organizations, political and research agendas, and networks. Of course, this kind of specialization is both necessary and desirable because the questions we need to ask and the approaches we develop for each may be quite distinct. However,

118

by positing the fields of bilingual and multicultural education as fundamentally different and unconnected ones, their common agendas are denied and each is left scrambling for limited resources. The unfortunate result is that proponents of bilingual and multicultural education sometimes become enemies with separate constituencies who know little about the other and may therefore respond with ignorance and hostility to one another.

Teachers need to understand that bilingual education is part and parcel of multicultural education. By allowing these two fields to be isolated from one another, the natural links between them are obscured. Language is one of the most salient aspects of culture. If the languages students speak, with all their attendant social meanings and affirmations, are either negated or relegated to a secondary position in their schooling, the possibility of school failure is increased. Because language and culture are so intimately connected, and because both bilingual and multicultural approaches seek to involve and empower the most vulnerable students in our schools, it is essential that we foster their natural links. This is not to imply that either bilingual or multicultural education is reserved for particular groups. On the contrary, both should be understood as necessary for *all* students. Nevertheless, given their roots and historical context, it is true that they began as responses to demands for improving the education of African American, Latino, American Indian, and Asian American students.

Redefining the Benefits of Linguistic Diversity

Generally speaking, programs that meet the needs of language-minority students require the separation of these students from others. In fact, the dilemma posed by this kind of isolation has been seen as one of the knottiest questions facing the proponents of bilingual education. Walter Landry (1983) has maintained that while the problems of race, class, gender, and disability discrimination are best resolved by integration, quite the opposite is true for language discrimination. That is, bilingual education demands the opportunity to *separate* students, at least for part of their education. This makes it particularly troublesome in a democratic society that purports to afford all students an equal educational opportunity. While this claim of equal education is far from real, it is nevertheless an important ideal to strive for. Thus, we need to face the dilemma of segregation that bilingual education presupposes.

There are several ways that the needs of limited English-proficiency and monolingual English speakers can be served simultaneously. One is through two-way bilingual education, as previously mentioned. Other approaches include setting aside times for joint instruction and for developing bilingual options within desegregation plans and magnet schools. Much remains to be done in expanding these options. Perhaps the most important shift in thinking that needs to take place is a new perception of bilingual classrooms, teachers, and students as a rich resource for nonbilingual classrooms, teachers, and students. When this shift happens, our schools will have taken the first step in commiting society to making bilingualism and even multilingualism central educational goals for *all* students. This is hardly the case right now. For language-minority students, for example, English language acquisition, often at the expense of their native language, is the primary goal rather than bilingualism. Even for our monolingual English students, the goal of bilingualism is an elusive one because foreign language courses are delayed until secondary school and are often ineffective. However, when language diversity becomes a benefit to all, we can be quite sure that the persistent underfunding of bilingual education will be eliminated and all students will benefit as a result.

We also need to mention, however, that bilingual education and other support services need to be understood as ensuring educational equity, particularly for language-minority students. The issue is not simply one of language; it goes much deeper. Bilingual education is a civil-rights issue because it provides one of the few guarantees that children who do not speak English will be educated in a language they understand. Given the increasing number of students who enter schools speaking a language other than English, it is clear that bilingual education will become even more important in the years ahead. Just as desegregation has been considered an important, and as yet unattained, civil right for those doomed to receive an inferior education because of inequality of resources, bilingual education is understood by language-minority communities as an equally important civil right. Thus, in expanding the framework for linguistic diversity so that all students can benefit from it, we need to remind ourselves that for students with limited English proficiency, bilingual education is not a frill, but *basic* education.

NATIVE LANGUAGE AND SCHOOL ACHIEVEMENT

Because language diversity has so often been viewed as a deficit, the positive influences of knowing a language other than English have frequently been overlooked (Cummins 1989, Hakuta 1986). Nevertheless, some recent research has examined the role of a native language other than English on the literacy development and academic achievement of students. I must stress that the lack of English skills alone does little to explain the poor academic achievement of students classified as limited in their English proficiency. For example, Cuban students have the highest educational levels of all Latinos, yet they are also the most likely to speak Spanish at home (Valdivieso and David 1988). Cubans are also the most highly educated and upwardly mobile of all Latino groups. It is clear, then, that speaking Spanish is not the problem. Rather, how language is viewed by the school and the larger society, how students themselves feel about their language, and most importantly, the economic class and professional background of parents all play key roles in the academic performance of students.

Given this caveat, nonetheless, research suggests that native-language maintenance seems to improve rather than jeopardize academic achievement. A study by David Dolson (1985), for example, found that students who used Spanish at home academically surpassed those peers whose families had switched to only English. Clearly, the home language of these students gave them a distinct advantage in learning. Another study found that recent Mexican immigrants were more successful in school in the United States than were long-time Mexican American residents. The same has been found with recent Puerto Rican arrivals as compared with those who have been here through all or most of their schooling (Matute-Bianchi 1986; Prewitt-Diaz 1983). Thus, the longer they are here, the worse their academic achievement. A major study of immigrant and nonimmigrant students in San Diego, California, had similar findings. They concluded that Latino, Filipino, and Asian immigrants who were just becoming fluent in English were more academically successful than their United States-born counter-parts (Rumbaut and Ima 1987). Clearly, then, language differences are not the major problem.

Other recent research bolster these findings. For example, studies by Luis Moll and Stephen Díaz (1987) on successful reading and writing learning environments for Latino students found that the students' native language and culture did not handicap their learning. Instead, they concluded that the problems language-minority students face are generally due to instructional arrangements in schools that fail to capitalize on the strengths, including linguistic and cultural resources, that they bring to school. In her research with four Mexican American students, Nancy Commins (1989) also found that the classroom setting for language-minority students can work as an interven-ing variable to support or to weaken students' perceptions of themselves and can thus contribute to their linguistic and academic development or lack of it. In fact, one of the major themes demonstrated by the student profiles was the ambivalence they experienced about their bilingualism.

Thus, speaking a language other than English is not necessarily a handicap; on the contrary, it can be a great asset to learning. The real issue is how such language use is interpreted. For example, bilingual and other support services for students with limited English proficiency frequently have a low status. Even their physical placement within schools is indicative of this. These programs are often found in large, windowless closets, in hallways, or in classrooms next to the boiler room. It is not surprising, then, that even the parents of children in these programs press for a quick exit for their children.

Yet, the fact is that bilingual education and other programs that support native-language use, even if only as a transition to English, are generally more effective than programs such as English as a Second Language (ESL) alone. This is true not only in terms of learning content in the native language, but in learning *English* as well. This seemingly contradictory finding can be understood if one considers the fact that students in bilingual programs are provided with continued education in content areas *along with* structured instruction in English. In addition, they are building on their previous literacy and thus it becomes what W.E. Lambert (1975) has called an *additive* form of bilingual education. *Subtractive* bilingual education, on the other hand, occurs when one language is substituted for another, and true literacy is not achieved in either. This often happens in programs where the students' native language is eliminated and English grammar, phonics, and other language features are taught out of context with the way in which real day-to-day language is used.

Even in programs where English is not used or used minimally, results show dramatic gains in students' achievement. Jim Campos and Robert Keatinge (1988), for example, found that Latino children enrolled in a Spanish-only preschool program developed more skills that would prepare them for school than children in a bilingual preschool program where the main goal was to develop proficiency in English. A comparative evaluation of bilingual and ESL-only programs also found that students in bilingual programs consistently outperformed those in ESL-only programs, *even* in their English-language performance (Crawford 1988). Ironically, the more native-language instruction students received, the better they performed in English. It is clear, then, that even if the primary purpose of education in our society is to learn English (a debatable position at best), bilingual programs seem to work more effectively than their English-only counterparts because bilingual programs use students' acquired literacy as the basis for learning English. These findings have been consistently reported by researchers who work in the field of bilingual education. Thus, when students' language is used as the basis for their education, when it is respected and valued, students tend to succeed in school (Krashen and Biber 1988; Heath 1986; Edelsky 1989).

A number of studies point to the same conclusions in respect to culture. For example, in a study of successful Punjabi students, Margaret Gibson (1987) found that parents consistently admonished their children to maintain their culture and made it clear that not doing so would dishonor their families and communities. In addition, a major study of Southeast Asian students found an intriguing connection between grades and culture: Higher grade-point averages were positively related to the maintenance of traditional values, ethnic pride, and close social and cultural ties with members of the same ethnic group (Rumbaut and Ima 1987).

In my own research (Nieto 1992) with academically successful students, I found that maintaining language and culture were essential in supporting and sustaining their academic achievement. In a series of in-depth interviews with these linguistically, culturally, and economically diverse students, one of the salient features that accounted for school success was a strong-willed determination to hold onto their culture and native language. Their pride in culture and language, however, was not without conflict. That is, most of these young people expressed both pride and shame in their culture. Given the assimilationist messages of our society, this is hardly surprising. What was surprising, however, was the steadfastness with which they maintained their culture and language in spite of such messages. Yet, for the most part, these were students who would not be expected to succeed in school given their disadvantaged economic position.

What can we learn, then, from research that focuses on the importance of language and culture in the academic achievement of students? One intriguing conclusion is that the more students are involved in resisting assimilation by maintaining their culture and language, the more successful they will be in school. That is, cultural and linguistic maintenance seem to have a positive impact on academic success. This is obviously not true in all cases: We can all think of examples of people who have felt they had to assimilate in order to succeed in school. The case of Richard Rodriguez (Rodriguez 1982), who felt compelled to choose between what he considered "public" and "private" worlds, comes to mind. That is, in order for him to succeed, he felt that he needed to reject his Mexican culture and the Spanish language. We can legitimately ask, however, whether his success represents a healthy one; for in the bargain, he lost part of himself.

While it is important not to overstate that linguistic and cultural maintenance seem to have a positive impact on academic achievement, it is nevertheless a real possibility and one that greatly challenges the melting pot ideology that has dominated U.S. schools and society throughout this century. The notion that assimilation is a necessary prerequisite for success in school and society is severely tested by current research.

We can even say that when their language and culture are reinforced not only at home but in school as well, students seem to develop less confusion and ambiguity about their ability to learn. Thus, regardless of the sometimes harsh attacks on their culture and language—as is the case in communities that have strident campaigns to pass English-only legislation—students whose language and culture are valued within the school setting pick up affirming messages about their worth.

IMPLICATIONS FOR CLASSROOM PRACTICE

The conclusion that maintaining native language and culture positively influences student achievement contradicts not only conventional educational philosophy, but also the policies and practices of schools that have done everything possible to eradicate students' culture and language in order, they maintain, for all students to succeed in school. The implications of this conclusion for classroom practice would mean that rather than attempting to erase culture and language, schools should do everything in their power to use, affirm, and maintain them as a foundation for students' academic success. It would mean establishing school policies and practices that stress cultural pride; that build on students' native-language ability; and that use the experiences, culture, and history of the students' communities as a basis for instruction.

If we move our thinking from *language diversity as deficit* to *language diversity as asset*, the implications for policy and practice become quite different from what they are currently (see chart on next two pages). Three key implications become clear. We must (1) strengthen bilingual programs, (2) develop a comprehensive multicultural education in which language diversity is an essential part, and (3) actively seek ways to involve the parents of language-minority students in their children's education. Let us briefly review each of these.

Bilingual Programs Need to Be Strengthened

Bilingual education has always been a controversial program within U.S. schools, especially during the past 25 years when it has become such an important option for students with limited English proficiency. It is clear that a rethinking of the very goals of bilingual education needs to take place in order to reinforce the crucial role it has proven to have in supporting both

(Chart 1)

LANGUAGE DIVERSITY AS DEFICIT

Assumptions:

Monolingualism is an asset.

Implications for Policy and Practice:

- "Sink or swim" language policies
- Native language elimination
- Integration at the expense of language-minority students
- "English-Only" policies in schools and communities

Knowing a language other than English is a hindrance to academic and social mobility.

- Transitional-style bilingual programs with "quick-exit" policies
- Other "compensatory" programs to help wipe out native language: special education, Chapter I, remedial English
- School curricula in all subject areas that promote an assimilationist, Eurocentric, and English-language ideal
- Low expectations for students who speak a language other than English
- Parents and community viewed as obstacles to children's learning.

(Chart 2)

LANGUAGE DIVERSITY AS ASSET

Assumptions:	Implications for Policy and Practice:
Bilingualism and multilingualism are assets.	• Maintenance/enrichment bilingual programs • Hiring policies that emphasize language diversity as essential and highly valued for staff and administrators • Classroom curricula, materials, and environment that reflect linguistic diversity • Classes offered in more than one language • Letters sent home reflect the language diversity of the school • More open communication with students, parents, and their communities considered essential • Bilingual classrooms, teachers, and students are rich educational resources for other classrooms, teachers, and students
Knowing a language other than English will promote academic and social mobility.	• Using students' native language for continued literacy development • Two-way bilingual programs • Students' native language is used as a valuable resource in the school and classroom communities, whether in bilingual classes or not • High expectations for students who speak a language other than English • Parents and community are an important asset to children's learning.

128

English acquisition and native language maintenance. Thus, not only should these programs be promoted, but they should also be accorded more visibility and respect within schools. This requires at least the following:

- more funding for bilingual programs,
- availability of such programs for all students with limited English proficiency,
- changing the "quick-exit" mentality of bilingual programs,
- more two-way programs in which bilingualism is promoted for all students.

Comprehensive Multicultural Programs Should Be Developed

Perceiving language diversity as an essential component of multicultural education means that the way in which schools view multicultural education needs to be changed. Multicultural education in many schools is reduced to a "Holidays-and-Heroes" approach where making exotic masks, eating ethnic foods, and commemorating "safe" heroes are the primary activities. Nevertheless, the research reviewed here has made clear that if culture and language are to be respected and affirmed, a comprehensive approach to multicultural education needs to be developed. This means that linguistic differences of students not in bilingual programs need to be respected as well. In fact, most students who speak a language other than English are not in bilingual programs, at least not for most of their schooling. Strategies that would send these students the message that their language is important and worthy of respect might include:

- encouraging students to use their native language with language peers, both in academic and social situations,
- pairing students with a buddy more fluent in English and encouraging each to teach the other,
- motivating students to teach their peers about their language and culture,

129

- inviting guests who speak a variety of languages to the classroom,
- using bilingual classrooms as a valuable resource for nonbilingual classrooms.

In addition, teachers who learn at least a working knowledge of one or more languages are telling their students that they appreciate the difficult work it takes to learn another language.

Parent Involvement of Language-Minority Students Should Be Promoted

The key role that parent involvement plays in the education of all students has been proven time and again (Henderson 1987). In the case of language-minority students, this role can be even more central. That is, because the parents of these children are often directly involved in their native-language literacy, their support of and participation in native-language maintenance are crucial. Although parents are the first and most important teachers of their children, the secondary status accorded to parents of language-minority students has impacted negatively on their involvement in school. Schools and teachers need to develop strategies that welcome parents as important partners in the education of their children. This means seeking ways to involve them both in and out of school, and to reaffirm the role they have in nurturing and maintaining children's literacy in their native language. One way of respecting their languages as languages of knowledge and learning is to use them in activities that promote literacy both in school and at home. This reasoning was behind the literacy project developed by Alma Ada (1988) in her research with Mexican American parents. Working with the parents of young elementary school children, she initiated a discussion-oriented project on children's literature. In the process of dialogue, reading, and writing, parents developed confidence and greater abilities in using the resources at their command, particularly their language and culture, to promote the literacy of their children. It is obvious from such research that parents can have a decisive effect on their children's literacy development and on their academic success in general. Schools need to acknowledge this important role and to seek innovative strategies to use the talents, hope, and motivation of parents in constructive ways. The view that poor parents and those who speak a language other than English are unable to provide appropriate environments for their children can lead to condescending practices that reject the skills and resources that parents do have.

CONCLUSION

Language is one of the fundamental signs of our humanity. It is "the palette from which people color their lives and culture. Intimately connected to the human experience, language oils the gears of social interactions and solidifies the ephemera of the mind into literature, history, and collective knowledge" (Allman 1990). While linguistic diversity is a fact of life in American schools and society, many languages are not given the respect and visibility they deserve. Because English is the language of power in our society, monolingualism is perceived as an asset. Those who speak a language other than English are generally viewed as having a problem that must be solved. At the core of such perceptions are racist and ethnocentric ideas about the value of some languages and not others.

Given recent trends in immigration, the shrinking of our world, and the subsequent necessity to learn to communicate with larger numbers of people, it is clear that a reconceptualization of the role of languages other than English within our schools and society in general has to take place. Such a reconceptualization needs to have the following components:

- a redefinition of linguistic diversity that views it as an asset rather than a deficit,
- policies and practices that build on students' strengths,

131

including their language and culture, rather than tearing these resources down,

- a desire to involve parents and other community people who represent the linguistic diversity our students bring to school,
- an understanding that bilingual education and other language approaches and services are important and necessary components of multicultural education, and
- an awareness that all students can benefit from linguistic diversity, not only those with limited English proficiency.

Given this kind of reconceptualization, the current policies and practices of schools need to be re-examined. Those that build on students' diversity should be strengthened, while those that focus on differences as deficits should be eliminated. This means, at the very least, that bilingual and multicultural programs *for all students* have to be comprehensively defined, adequately funded, and strongly supported.

REFERENCES

Ada, A.F. 1988. The Pajaro Valley experience. In *Minority language: From shame to struggle*, edited by T. Skutnabb-Kangas and J. Cummins. Clevedon, England: Multilingual Matters, Ltd.

Allman, W.F. 1990. The mother tongue. *U.S. News and World Report* 5 November 1990.

Campos, S. J. and Keatinge, H.R. 1988. The carpinteria language minority student experience: From theory, to practice, to success. In *Minority language: From shame to struggle*, edited by T. Skutnabb-Kangas and J. Cummins. Clevedon, England: Multilingual Matters, Ltd.

Castellanos, D. 1983. *The best of two worlds*. Trenton, N.J.: State Department of Education.

Collier, V.P. 1989a. How long? A synthesis of research on academic achievement in a second language. *TESOL Quarterly* 23 (3): 509–31.

Collier, V.P. 1989b. Academic achievement, attitudes, and occupations among graduates of two-way bilingual classes. Paper presented at the annual meeting of the American Educational Research Association. San Francisco, Calif.

Commins, N.L. 1989. Language and affect: Bilingual students at home and at school. *Language Arts* 66 (1): 29–43.

Crawford, J. 1988. Study challenges "model" ESL program's effectiveness. Report of study done by Virginia P. Collier and Wayne P. Thomas. *Education Week* 27 April 1988.

Cummins, J. 1989. *Empowering minority students.* Sacramento, Calif.: California Association for Bilingual Education.

Cummins, J. 1984. *Bilingualism and special education.* Clevedon, England: Multilingual Matters, Ltd.

Cummins, J. 1981. The role of primary language development in promoting educational success for language minority students. In *Schooling and language minority students: A theoretical framework,* Office of Bilingual Bicultural Education. Sacramento, Ca.: Evaluation, Dissemination, and Assessment Center, California State University, Los Angeles.

Daniel, H.A., ed. 1990. *Not only English: Affirming America's multilingual heritage.* Urbana, Ill.: National Council of Teachers of English.

Dolson, D.P. 1985. The effects of Spanish home language use on the scholastic performance of Hispanic pupils. *Journal of Multilingual and Multicultural Development* 6 (2): 135–56.

Edelsky, C. 1989. Bilingual children's writing: Fact and fiction. In *Richness in writing: Empowering ESL students,* edited by D.M. Johnson and D. H. Roen. New York: Longman Publishers.

Feistristzer, E.E. 1986. *Teacher crisis: Myth or reality? A state-by-state analysis.* Washington, DC: National Center for Education Information.

Gibson, M.A. 1987. The school performance of immigrant minorities: A comparative view. *Anthropology and Education Quarterly* 18 (4): 262–75.

Giles, H.; Scherer, K.R.; and Taylor, D.M. 1979. Speech markers in social interaction. In *Social markers in speech*, edited by K.R. Scherer and H. Giles. Cambridge, England: Cambridge University Press.

Hakuta, K. 1986. *Mirror of language: The debate on bilingualism.* New York: Basic Books.

Haugen, E. 1987. The language of imperialism: Unity or pluralism? In *Language of inequality*, edited by N. Wolfson and J. Manes. New York: Mouton Publishers.

Heath, S.B. 1986. Sociocultural contexts of language development. In *Beyond language: Social and cultural factors in schooling language minority students*, Office of Bilingual Education, California State Department of Education. Los Angeles, Ca.: Evaluation, Dissemination, and Assessment Center.

Henderson, A.T. 1987. *The evidence continues to grow: Parent involvement improves student achievement.* Columbia, Md.: National Coalition of Citizens in Education.

Hurtado, A. and Rodriguez, R. 1989. Language as a social problem: The repression of Spanish in south Texas. *Journal of Multilingual and Multicultural Development* 10 (5): 401–19.

Keller, G.S. and van Hooft, K.S. 1982. A chronology of bilingualism and bilingual education in the United States. In *Bilingual education for Hispanic students in the United States*, edited by J. Fishman and G. Keller. New York: Teachers College Press.

Kellogg, J.B. 1988. Forces of change. *Phi Delta Kappan* November 1988, 199–204.

Krashen, S. and Biber, D. 1988. *On course: Bilingual education's success in California.* Sacramento, Calif.: California Association for Bilingual Education.

Lambert, W.E. 1975. Culture and language as factors in learning and education. In *Education of immigrant students*, edited by A. Wolfgang. Toronto: OISE.

Landry, W.J. 1983. Future *Lau* regulations: Conflict between language rights and racial nondiscrimination. In *Theory, technology, and public policy on bilingual education*, edited by R.V. Padilla. Rosslyn, Va.: National Clearinghouse for Bilingual Education.

Lau v. Nichols 414 U.S. 563. 1974. St. Paul, Minn.: West Publishing Co. Language discrimination was the basis for the unanimous Supreme Court decision in *Lau v. Nichols.*

Matute-Bianchi, M.E. 1986. Ethnic identities and patterns of school success and failure among Mexican-descent and Japanese American students in a California high school: An ethnographic analysis. *American Journal of Education* 15 (1): 233–55.

Moll, L.C. and Díaz, S. 1987. Change as the goal of educational research. *Anthropology and Education Quarterly* 18 (4): 300–11.

Muller, T. and Espenshade, T. 1985. *The fourth wave.* Washington, DC: Urban Institute Press.

National Association of Teachers of English. 1990. English plus: Issues in bilingual education. *Annals of the American Academy of Political and Social Science* 508.

National Coalition of Advocates for Students (NCAS). 1988. *New voices: Immigrant students in U.S. public schools.* Boston: NCAS.

National Education Association. 1988. *Official English/English only: More than meets the eye.* Washington, DC: National Education Association.

Natriello, G.; McDill, E.L.; and Pallas, A.M. 1990. *Schooling disadvantaged children: Racing against catastrophe.* New York: Teachers College Press.

Nieto, S. 1992. *Affirming diversity: The sociopolitical context of multicultural education.* New York: Longman Publishers.

Ovando, C.J. and Collier, V.P. 1985. *Bilingual and ESL classrooms: Teaching in multicultural contexts.* New York: McGraw-Hill Book Co.

Phillipson, R. 1988. Linguicism: Structures and ideologies in linguistic imperialism. In *Minority language: From shame to struggle,* edited by T. Skutnabb-Kangas and J. Cummins. Clevedon, England: Multilingual Matters, Ltd.

Prewitt-Díaz, J.O. 1983. A study of self-esteem and school sentiment in two groups of Puerto Rican students. *Educational and Psychological Research* 3: 161–67.

Rodriguez, R. 1982. *Hunger and memory: The education of Richard Rodriguez*. Boston: David R. Godine.

Rumbaut, R.G. and Ima, K. 1987. *The adaptation of Southeast Asian refugee youth: A comparative study*. San Diego, Ca.: Office of Refugee Resettlement.

Skutnabb-Kangas, T. 1988. Multilingualism and the education of minority children. In *Minority language: From shame to struggle*, edited by T. Skutnabb-Kangas and J. Cummins, 13. Clevedon, England: Multilingual Matters, Ltd.

Sleeter, C.E. and Grant, C.A. 1988. A rationale for integrating race, gender, and social class. In *Class, races, and gender in American education*, edited by L. Weis. New York: State University of New York Press.

Valdivieso, R. and David, C. 1988. *U.S. Hispanics: Challenging issues for the 1990s*. Washington, DC: Population Trends and Public Policy.

Weinberg, M. 1977. *A chance to learn: A history of race and education in the U.S.* Cambridge, England: Cambridge University Press.

Chapter 9

REDUCING PREJUDICE IN SOCIETY: THE ROLE OF SCHOOLS

by Glenn S. Pate

Of all the formal agents in society, the schools are in the best position to prevent and reduce prejudice. By the time students leave school, their attitudes, beliefs, and behavior toward people are generally formed, and it will take extraordinary circumstances to bring about significant changes. Our task is made more difficult by the fact that children already have attitudes about other racial/ethnic groups when they start school. Thus, in many cases, we are not dealing with children with neutral opinions, but with children who hold negative attitudes before we even have our first opportunity to influence them.

We know that both prejudiced and nonprejudiced attitudes are taught and experienced. It is incumbent upon us to recognize these facts, deliberately plan a course of action, and accept our pivotal role in reducing prejudice. We begin by acknowledging that prejudice is still a problem in our society. We also must recognize the fact that there are differences among people and among groups. To be blind to these conditions is to be less than honest, and our students know it. We may not say that everyone is the same. Fortunately, there is a body of knowledge in this area that we can draw on. Our task, therefore, is to identify that knowledge and then to implement effective policies, programs, and practices that will reduce prejudice.

SCHOOL-WIDE CONSIDERATIONS

All of the school's policies and practices will be meaningless unless the adults in the school model appropriate attitudes and behaviors. Our position as role models is pivotal as we strive toward the reduction of prejudice. We must model, not just the acceptance of diversity, but also the embracing of it. If we merely indicate our tolerance for the differences among the students in the school, we are not going far enough. We must take joy and pride from the diversity. This includes our attitudes toward differences in dress, language, and cultural norms. If we are in a monocultural school or community, there are still differences among the students, and we can certainly recognize the diversity in American society and in the world. We also need to model our intolerance of any discriminatory or prejudiced behavior. This includes a host of potential negative occurrences, such as name-calling, acts of exclusion, and ethnic jokes. Whenever we accept an ethnic joke without challenging the culprit, we are joining the ranks of the bigots.

Schools must establish and make public their policies of antidiscrimination and antiprejudice. These policies will be based on democratic principles, equal opportunity, and a sense of fair play. They must be known by the people in the school, adults as well as students, and by the community. The policies must be living and dynamic rather than a set of statements hidden in a manual or in a report submitted to an accreditation agency. Schools must also take care to insure that the policies and rules are enforced fairly. This means not only trying to be fair, but also conducting research periodically to determine if inequities do in fact exist. And imagine the sense of ownership that could occur if students and members of the community were involved in developing these policies.

Some specific and fairly obvious practices with which the schools must be constantly concerned invoke a sense of fair play. Great care must be taken to avoid using culturally biased examinations and examination procedures. The schools should guard against any particular group of students dominating functions such as clubs or teams. Of course, care must be taken to avoid using biased textbooks or other educational materials. The types of assemblies or special functions should be examined to insure cultural and gender fairness. Notice the awards and special recognitions that are given to students. Are there cultural or gender imbalances? We also need to take into consideration differences in student learning-styles. When we assume that all students prefer the same type of learning environment and have the same cognitive styles of processing information, we are not being very intelligent nor equitable. As discussed in detail elsewhere in this book, it is simply unfair to force all students to learn in the same way.

A practice fairly common in schools that interferes with the reduction of prejudice is tracking. Not only has tracking failed to achieve desired academic results, it clearly segregates the students (Slavin 1987). Tracking, either between classes or within a class, promotes a separation among the students and leads to stereotyping. It is difficult to imagine a school that has a successful prejudice-reduction program also practicing tracking.

Regardless of how well-intentioned it may be in combating prejudice, a school must be constantly vigilant in examining its own practices and the results of its efforts. James Lynch (1987) gives us a thorough set of checklists that cover the areas of governance, policy statement, staffing, communications, resources, language, rules and regulations, extracurricular activities, staff development, curriculum and teaching methods, assessment policy, and multicultural educational policy.

Leslie Hegert and Raymond Rose (1986) also provide us with a component checklist for the school level and one for the classroom level. For each variable assessed, they give us descriptions of practices that are ideal, acceptable, and unacceptable. Schools that regularly use either of the above sets of checklists are virtually guaranteed to be aware of inequities and inappropriate practices.

In the same vein, Carolyn Murray and Reginald Clark (1990) recommend that schools engage in self-examination. They have identified eight ways racism may be subtly present in a school: through the forms of hostile and insensitive acts, bias in the use of harsh sanctions, bias in giving active attention to students, bias in selection of curriculum materials, inequality in the amount of instruction, bias in attitude toward students, failure to hire racial-minority teachers and other personnel, and denial of racist actions.

An intriguing self-examination was conducted in Ann Arbor, Michigan (Polakow-Suransky and Ulaby, 1990). High school students there developed a questionnaire to assess racism in their own school. The results of the survey led to positive changes that improved the learning environment.

A very positive aspect of our efforts to reduce prejudice is its relation to effective education in general. When we exercise appropriate prejudice-reducing practices, we also do the things that result in a better education for all students. Notice this consistency in the summaries below.

R.A. Kyle (1985) identified these characteristics of effective schools:

- a school climate conducive to learning;
- teachers' expectations that all students can achieve;
- an emphasis on basic-skills instruction and quality time on task for learners;
- a system of clear instructional objectives for the monitoring and evaluation of learning;
- a head teacher who creates incentives for learning, sets school goals, maintains discipline, observes classrooms and is a strong leader.

In summarizing data regarding effective desegregation in high schools, Robert Slavin and Nancy Madden (1979), identified these factors as contributing to positive race relations:

- teaching methods that are intended to improve race relations,
- principals who are highly rated by their teachers as supportive of all teachers,
- positive racial attitudes held by teachers and principals,
- institutional support for integration,
- low conflict and tension.

Similarly, Del Stover (1990) interviewed a large number of knowledgeable people in the field of prejudice reduction and made the following recommendations:

- Adopt a firm policy of zero tolerance for racism in any form.
- Consider positive message systems such as awards programs.
- Expand social contacts among cultural groups.
- Investigate in-service opportunities on prejudice for teachers and administrators.
- Add multicultural education programs to the curriculum.

Of course, readers of this book will recognize that multicultural programs should not be "add-on" programs, but an integral part of the schooling. The major point, however, is that practices that promote effective education also promote prejudice reduction.

One of the most pressing concerns for many schools regarding relations among groups of students is found in schools that are desegregated. Several summative studies (Garcia 1989) have concluded that desegregation *per se* has not had the desired results of reducing prejudice. While a complete analysis of desegregation is beyond the scope of this chapter, it certainly is a relevant topic. It may be that the failure of desegregation to reduce prejudice is the result of too many people in too many schools not giving proper consideration to the social-contact theory. This theory was first put forth by the parent of the study of prejudice, Gordon Allport (1954), and it has since been expanded upon and refined by others. Briefly, it maintains that contact between different groups of people will have beneficial effects *if* certain conditions are met. The requisite conditions are:

- There is an opportunity for the people involved to get to know one another as individuals.
- The individuals in the two groups have equal status in

the situations.
- The people have common interests and are similar in characteristics such as age or occupation.
- The social norms (and the authority figures) are favorable to association between the two groups.
- The circumstances of the situation favor cooperation, or at least do not introduce competition or conflict.
- The people have common goals and the presence or activities of members of the two groups help in the achievement of the individuals' goals, or at least do not present an obstacle. (Selltiz and Cook 1963)

Without belaboring the point, it does seem that if school personnel worked effectively to create the requisite conditions for the social-contact theory, our desegregation efforts would have a much greater impact on reducing prejudice.

THE TEACHERS

Teachers are people, too; and like all people, they may have their own prejudices. The mores in society have evolved to the point that in most social situations, and in virtually all professional functions, prejudiced teachers are reluctant to express their biases. These people may be closet bigots within their own classroom; still other teachers who possess a sense of fair play or a sense of propriety may be undiscriminating bigots. No degree of persuasion or exhortation will affect their beliefs or attitudes. Of course, self-examination or honest introspection may help these people change, but there must be extreme circumstances present to make true change desirable in their minds. In the psychological view, they will not change unless they want to change. Perhaps the most likely endeavor that would help alter these perceptions is for the prejudiced teachers to conduct an in-depth study of the phenomena of prejudice. We will discuss this approach later in terms of reducing student prejudice.

In order to effectively work with students from various backgrounds, the teacher must have a good understanding of the students' cultures. Without this knowledge, the teacher will not only be a less-than-effective instructor, but will be susceptible to false impressions and stereotypes. The teacher must also be knowledgeable about cultures not represented in his or her classroom. This is especially important for people who work in a largely monocultural school. The teacher must be armed with accurate and current information, not only to avoid making mistakes and overgeneralizations, but also to help students identify stereotypes and inaccuracies that may appear in educational materials or films used. The teacher must display an honest inquiry and respect for the truth.

When teaching, most of us are generally unaware of particular interaction patterns that may be occurring. There is evidence that teachers show partiality toward students based on factors such as a student's race, ethnicity, gender, appearance, and seating location (Motta and Vane 1977; Rist 1970; Wilkinson and Marrett 1985). If we are unaware of our inequitable treatment, the bias-based behavior will continue. Teachers need to systematically and objectively study their interactions with students. A teacher may want to enlist the aid of a colleague to make observations by using some of the many observational tools that are available. Thomas Good and Jere Brophy (1991) have identified several such instruments. Using an observational instrument in conjunction with a videotape makes a clear and powerful mirror. We can, and should, use this mirror so that we may work with our students in a more equitable manner.

One of the simplest and most effective practices a teacher can follow to reduce student prejudice is to develop a way of viewing other groups. It is imperative that we see a particular group not as a whole, but as comprised of individuals. While the individuals share characteristics that give them membership in the group, they are still unique individuals. The teacher must have and must develop in students the mental habit of

143

differentiating among people within a given group. The groups in question will be as diverse as Jews, Russians, Republicans, New Yorkers, or bird-watchers. Differences in characteristics, attitudes, beliefs, and behaviors of individuals within a group must be recognized; otherwise, we are stereotyping. We must correct students when they use such absolutes as "all," "none," and "always," and help them think more clearly by using such terms as "some," "most," or "some of the time." Perhaps we do differentiate against groups when we fail to differentiate among members of those groups.

A study (Roberts 1985) in the elementary grades that examined degrees of integration and interracial friendship patterns found that certain teachers consistently had the highest rates of integration. Those teachers recommended these strategies:

- Be optimistic about the performance of all students.

- Have high expectations for the success of all students.

- Treat all students equally.

- Establish a classroom climate that minimizes tension and anxiety.

- Be consistent and fair in discipline.

We note again that these recommendations are consistent with recommendations for effective teaching in general.

TEACHING STRATEGIES

We do have some knowledge about particular teaching approaches that may lead to a reduction of student prejudice. Each strategy has certain potential advantages and desired outcomes as well as certain constraints or required conditions. Simply employing a particular strategy will not inevitably result in a reduction in prejudice. We must take care to use the strategy in a thoughtful, careful manner; otherwise, we will be disappointed in the results.

144

Ironically, the most obvious approach is the least effective. We may refer to this approach as a direct, head-on antiprejudice attack. If we devise an antiprejudice unit designed to make students like each other better, we are likely to have unwanted results. Students tend to see this approach as propaganda intended to manipulate them, and they will resist. In fact, some studies have found this approach to actually increase the level of prejudice. Exhortation and sermonizing simply do not work.

A better approach is to study the phenomena of prejudice from an outsider's view. That is, we can study prejudice in the manner an anthropologist may study a village or the way a sociologist may study certain social phenomena. This places the students outside the target of the study so they do not feel threatened or manipulated. Studies that have used this approach have had positive, prejudice-reducing results. This is the approach referred to earlier for teachers who harbor prejudiced attitudes.

One of the most exciting and effective approaches is the use of cooperative learning. Extensive research conducted with the various forms of cooperative learning consistently demonstrate beneficial results. Whether the version used has been Jigsaw, Teams, Games, Tournaments and Student Teams, Academic Divisions, or Group Investigation, students benefit in important ways. Not only do their interracial and cross-gender friendship patterns increase, they develop a stronger sense of self-esteem, a more positive attitude toward school, and a more internal locus of control. They also experience an increase in academic achievement. We notice again the consistency between practices that reduce prejudice and those that promote effective education.

When we recognize that prejudice is intellectually unsound, it seems reasonable to attack prejudice by increasing students' cognitive skills. Such efforts have proven to be effective. This approach means much more than merely teaching information. Facts do not speak for themselves, but rather are interpreted sometimes inaccurately by each individual. We also have the tendency to focus on those facts that support our previously held convictions and to ignore those that contradict our beliefs. Therefore, this approach refers to an increase in students' critical-thinking skills and how they process information.

According to Walsh (1988), "Thinking critically is the antithesis of prejudiced thinking. Thinking critically begins with being disposed to question, to examine, to suspend judgment until the available evidence is weighed." Given this, promoting students' cognitive skills and critical thinking abilities is appropriate for all subjects and grade levels and pays high dividends. A specific example of this would be teaching democratic principles in a social studies class at any grade level. Students should know the Bill of Rights and the principles by which our society protects individual citizens. If students are unaware that a person's rights are being violated, they will not see a problem and cannot speak against discrimination. Teachers, however, can remedy this ignorance.

A theory that seeks to synthesize several theories on the causes of prejudices and various approaches for remediation is the *Defenses to Prejudice Theory* (Pate 1985). This theory holds that each of us is exposed to prejudiced thinking throughout our lives, and the exposure is especially important during our formative years. Some of us are greatly influenced by this experience and become prejudiced people. Others, due to potential areas of psychological and intellectual strengths, reject all or most of the biased messages and do not become as prejudiced. The potential areas of defense that arm us so that we reject the prejudiced messages are: a strong self-concept, a positive view of people in general, a sense of fair play and acceptance of the democratic principles, and a clear reasoning ability. Research has demonstrated that students who have strong defenses, such as positive self-concept, are less prejudiced than students who have weaker defense systems. While we cannot prove a cause-and-effect relationship between these variables and level of prejudice, it does seem reasonable that teachers should pursue practices that help students achieve higher self-esteem, better reasoning abilities, a positive view of people, and a strong sense of fair play.

Many teachers have found appropriate audiovisual materials useful in influencing attitudes about prejudice. Films that have a racially integrated cast are more effective than those with leading characters represented by a single racial group. Films depicting real human struggles are more powerful than exhortation or propaganda films. Films in which students can participate vicariously as well as those that portray members of minority groups as real people with basic needs, hopes, dreams, and problems also affect students' perceptions.

As with film, the use of literature and special reading material can help lessen prejudice. Elementary and middle-school students are especially apt to identify with characters in a story, have an increased level of empathy, and come to recognize past stereotypes. Multicultural reading materials, biographies, and autobiographies are powerful and readily available vehicles for reducing prejudice. For example, the autobiographies of Maya Angelou, in addition to being fine literature, offer a rich and rewarding avenue toward changing students' attitudes.

CONCLUSION

Prejudice is still a problem in our society. Preventing and minimizing it are extremely complex and difficult tasks. The problem will not go away unless the schools make an active and thoughtful campaign against it. It appears, however, that too many educators have decided that the issues of prejudice have already been confronted and resolved.

As schools move toward effective and efficient teaching, it is easy to lose sight of their role as agents of prejudice reduction. However, we can mobilize our efforts, make a commitment, and draw upon present knowledge to make substantial changes in students' attitudes. Each person in the educational system has a role to play and can contribute.

As we make strides toward reducing prejudice, we will also be doing those things that promote more effective education in general. We need to have adults and students widen their concept of "we." The circle of "us" and "our group" and "our people" needs to increase in size so that it includes all people. As we work to extend our mental parameters, we not only help to eliminate prejudice in other people, we become better people ourselves.

REFERENCES

Allport, G.W. 1954. *The nature of prejudice.* Boston: Addison Wesley.

Garcia, A. 1989. Just when you thought it was safe: Racism in the schools. *Educational Horizons* 67 (4): 156–62.

Good, T.L. and Brophy, J.E. 1991. *Looking in classrooms.* New York: Harper Collins.

Hegert, L. F. and Rose, R. 1986. Measuring equity in education. *Equity and Excellence* 22 (4), (6):58–63.

Kyle, R.A., ed. 1985. Reaching for excellence: An effective school source book. In *Prejudice reduction and the schools*, edited by J. Lynch. New York: Nichols Publishing Co., 1987.

Lynch, J., ed. 1987. *Prejudice reduction and the schools.* New York: Nichols Publishing Co.

Motta, R. and Vane, J. 1977. An investigation of teacher perceptions of sex-typed behaviors. *Journal of Education Research* 69: 363–68.

Murray, C.B. and Clark, R. M. 1990. Targets of racism. *The American School Board Journal* 177 (6): 22–24.

Pate, G.S. 1985. The defenses to prejudice theory. Paper presented to American Educational Research Association, Chicago.

Polakow-Suransky, S. and Ulaby, N. 1990. Students take action to combat racism. *Phi Delta Kappan* 71 (8): 601–6.

Rist, R. 1970. Student social class and teacher expectations: The self-fulfilling prophecy in ghetto education. *Harvard Educational Review* 40: 411–51.

Roberts, G.J. 1985. Classroom social structure analysis: A tool to help teachers foster integration. *Equity and Excellence* 22 (4), (6): 67–71.

Selltiz, C. and Cook, S.W. 1963. The effects of personal contact on intergroup relations. *Theory into Practice* II (3): 158–65.

Slavin, R.E. 1987. Grouping for instruction: Equity and effectiveness. *Equity and Excellence* 23 (1), (2): 31–36.

Slavin, R.E., and Madden, N.A. 1979. School practices that improve race relations. *American Educational Research Journal* 16 (2): 169–80.

Stover, D. 1990. The new racism. *The American School Board Journal* 177 (6): 14–18.

Walsh, D. 1988. Critical thinking to reduce prejudice. *Social Education* 52 (4): 280–82.

Wilkinson, L. and Marrett, C., eds. 1985. *Gender influences in classroom interaction.* New York: Academic Press.

Chapter 10

INVOLVING SPECIAL EDUCATORS IN CHALLENGING INJUSTICE IN EDUCATION

by Christine E. Sleeter and Constanz Hartney

What needs or issues related to multicultural education can special educators anticipate for the twenty-first century? Not being good forecasters ourselves, we examined the current literature to detect trends in the issues being discussed. Rather than finding trends, however, we found the same problems being discussed time after time. This led us to reconceptualize our main question: Given the continued existence of problems, what can special educators do to address them more effectively?

RECURRING ISSUES IN THE LITERATURE

The main issues related to multiculturalism that special educators discuss repeatedly are: (1) overrepresentation of students of color in special education, (2) assessment bias, (3) bias in placement decisions, and (4) identification of and service to language-minority students (Lynch and Lewis 1983; Maheady et al. 1984; Ortiz and Maldonado-Colon 1986; Smith 1983). Some articles describe these problems; some provide helpful suggestions for addressing them; and a few examine school districts that have dealt with them successfully. But it was alarmingly clear that although these issues of justice and equity were universally recognized, they remained largely unresolved. Students of color and students from low-income families continue to be placed disproportionately in special education, while they are underidentified as gifted. Language-minority students often continue to be regarded as language-deficient, or as a homogeneous population that should all be served in the same way.

The basic problem appears to be that schools are not structured to serve the interests of students of color, students from low-income backgrounds, or students whose first language is not English as well as they serve students who are white, native English speakers from middle- or upper-class backgrounds. Special education reflects this, and many special educators recognize it, but fixing special education will not solve what is wrong with general education.

For example, one of the main functions of schools is to sort students differentially for distinct and unequal roles in later life. Schools help identify who will go to college and who will not; who will go to prestigious universities and who will go to state or local colleges. This means that beginning with kindergarten, parents and communities compete to try to ensure their children access to a better life. To many general educators, special education and other remedial programs serve as a place to put students who are not keeping pace with the majority. And because the curriculum, teaching strategies, tests, expectations, and procedures for relating with parents that are used in schools as a whole are designed primarily by and work best for white, middle- to upper-class citizens—those with greatest social power—their children are most likely to meet standard requirements. As such, they will probably be identified as qualified for post-secondary opportunities and further education. Progressive educators have always protested such biases in the education system, and do occasionally win gains. But at the same time, they often see the playing field redrawn to ensure the same unequal outcomes.

Given these realities, conflicts surrounding dispropor-tionate placement, assessment bias, and language issues will increase as student populations become increasingly diverse and the lower class continues to grow. However, the problems will probably take on shifting guises: old categories in special and remedial education will be changed or disbanded, while new categories will be created.

151

For example, African American students have been and continue to be placed disproportionately in classes for the educable mentally retarded (EMR). Donald Macmillan, Irving Hendrick, and Alice Watkins (1988), for example, concluded on the basis of statistics from the early 1980s that in spite of legal challenges to disproportionate placement, "the figures continue to suggest an overrepresentation of Black children in EMR programs, even after full implementation of PL 94–142 (p. 427). However, because of objections to placement in this program, students of color are placed increasingly in other remedial programs. James Tucker (1980) found the proportion of African American students in classes for the mentally retarded dropped between 1970 and 1977, while at the same time it rose in classes for the learning disabled. Nationally between 1978 and 1984, the percentage of African American students identified as EMR dropped from 3.4 percent to 3.1 percent, while the percentage identified as learning disabled rose from 2.2 percent to 4.5 percent. The category of learning disabilities expanded greatly during this time period, so by 1984 it housed 4.2 percent of the total student-population (Stern 1987). We share Daniel Reschly's (1988) concern that "limiting, reducing, or eliminating overrepresentation in one kind of program . . . almost inevitably leads to overrepresentation in some other sort of special or remedial program" such as learning disabilities or Chapter I (p. 320).

The "excellence" movement of the 1980s gave rise to a new category, "at-risk" students, which some are beginning to use as a formal category for remedial students. But this is surely a new label for an old problem. This shifting of categories can lead many people to assume that old problems have been solved and that new problems are arising. But it really reflects the persistence of the same conflicting pressures that schools experience by serving a culturally diverse and stratified society.

The larger issue that must be examined is how a school system functions to help students of color get ahead as opposed to legitimizing their lower achievement. Jim Cummins (1988) distinguishes between processes that disable and those that empower minority students. For example, assessment devices, such as IQ tests and standardized achievement tests, disable students when they are used to "explain" why minority students are not performing well and to predict poor future performance. Richard Duran (1989) recommends curriculum-based assessment for the purpose of providing guidance in what to teach a student next, as opposed to IQ or standardized achievement tests that describe failure, but do not provide guidance for instruction. Curricula that are Eurocentric and exclude minority-group cultures are alienating to many students of color, as are instructional strategies that reward passive rather than active learning behavior. When schools systematically reorient themselves toward minority-group success and power, problems reflected in overrepresentation in special education will diminish. This larger systemic reorientation, however, constantly meets with resistance. Special and remedial educators often clearly recognize the problems, but they do not know what to do about them. One of us (Sleeter 1991) worked with a group of teachers in a multicultural education staff-development program, and found the specialists much more sensitive to the issues than many of the general education teachers. One teacher had developed a particularly sophisticated analysis of social injustices in education, which she described in an interview:

[I'm] seeing basically how our system is set up, the value system our whole society is set up on. And it makes me feel like we are here because of a lot of suffering. We are here where we are today. And that's very sad. It didn't need to be that way, but a lot of people have suffered to bring us the affluence that we have.

Her own experience as a special education teacher had bred anger at how the education system treats students assigned to her. In a paper she wrote about African American literature, she explained that, "Many cultures and governmental systems

153

have been established on the idea that some people were meant to rule and live in luxury and some were meant to serve and live in poverty and suffering." She was angry with "the system," but did not know what to do in response; sometimes she concluded expression of her frustration with, "I can't change everything."

If many special educators recognize that schools do not serve racial and cultural minority- and lower-class students well, what can they do to try to make a difference? We will discuss two related but different kinds of action educators can take. First, they need to learn to handle the stress brought about by injustices they see daily; and second, they need to learn to work together actively to confront injustices in their own schools and school districts.

MANAGING STRESS

Many teachers blame their failures on the stress and frustration they feel at facing an overwhelming task. They report lack of support from the administration and from their colleagues as far more frustrating than, for example, the difficulty of classroom management. Many special education teachers are vehement in proclaiming that they know what is required of them, but they feel unable to do that because of the extraordinary amount of stress they encounter on the job. Further, some of this stress results from injustices that special education teachers see students having to face. Stress will impair one's ability to teach as well as one's ability to confront injustices. The special educator must learn to manage stress at both a personal and professional level.

Stress has been defined as a nonspecific response of the body to any demand placed on it (Selye 1956). It should be understood that every demand made on the body is in some way specific because it is unique. For example, heat produces sweating, which is itself a highly specific response. Stress is not something that can be avoided, because at every moment in any organism's existence there are some demands placed on it in the form of life-maintaining functions.

Hans Selye identified two types of stress: eustress and distress. *Eustress* is seen as pleasant and curative. This type of stress is necessary to provide an organism with sufficient drive to continue life-sustaining activities. *Distress* is unpleasant and disease-producing; it is seen as dysfunctional. Both types of stress have the same physiological and psychological effect on the body in that both produce exhaustion. This component of stress is particularly relevant when discussing teacher burnout, a condition more frequently encountered by the special education teacher than the regular classroom teacher. Selye recognizes that during the stage of exhaustion, adaptability to a stressful situation is not infinite and that there are limits within which an organism functions in a highly individualized manner. If the stressor is sufficiently severe and prolonged, exhaustion follows. Although sleep and rest restore resistance and adaptability, they do not bring these to previous levels, so continued subjection to stress may result in complete exhaustion. That is, the individual suffers from burnout.

This may sound very familiar to special education teachers or other teachers who work in remedial programs, who find themselves trying to satisfy the various needs of their students that, to some extent, the school as a whole should be more actively helping to meet. Stress is compounded when the teacher tries to engage support and cooperation of others who would rather not deal with special education students.

Most individuals acquire their own spontaneous ways of dealing with stress. These strategies usually include the following: (1) removing unnecessary stressors; (2) not allowing certain neutral events to become stressors; (3) developing a proficiency in dealing with conditions that they do not want to, or cannot, avoid; and (4) seeking diversion from the demand. Other individuals develop certain response patterns as a way of coping with stressful stimuli. One such response pattern called *cognitive set* is particularly relevant to the teacher in the multicultural setting. According to stress theory, the individual develops a cognitive set in which irrational conclusions are drawn from stressful experiences (Ellis and Harper 1975).

Let us consider the following scenario. The teacher from the room next to the emotionally disturbed (ED) class appears at the door, obviously agitated.

> "Miss Jones, can you please keep your class quiet? We are trying to work next door, and we can't concentrate with all this noise. Besides, if these people can't be kept quiet, maybe they don't belong in this school."

> "I'm sorry, Miss Smith, I'll try my best to keep them quiet," replies Miss Jones, with a sigh, and thinking, "She's right, these kids are mostly Black; they don't belong in this school, so far from their neighborhood."

In this example, Miss Jones acquiesced to Miss Smith's belief that classrooms should be quiet, and she accepted the assumption that African American students are really intruders in the school. Instead, the more accurate conclusion would be that Miss Smith is right; these kids are noisy. But she should understand that they have learning styles that require classroom strategies that are somewhat noisy. Furthermore, the principal does not recognize this and therefore has made no arrangements to make sure that Miss Jones's class does not disrupt others.

Miss Jones has attempted to deal with her stress by tolerating things as they are and accepting blame for misconceived problems. It would be more constructive, from an equity perspective, if Miss Jones were to confront the situation. But first, she would need to develop other strategies for managing her own stress. The suggestions that follow provide some techniques that all teachers can use.

The most effective treatment orientation for stress in the clinical setting is claimed by behavior therapy. Joseph Wolpe

(1973) claims a 90 percent improved or cured rate. The most widely used treatment strategy today for stress is a cognitive-behavioral approach, which assumes that learning is more than merely automatic and that some cognitive processing is also operative (Meichenbaum 1972). In other words, human learning involves thinking about what is learned along with the observable behavioral changes. Strategies that would be most useful for the special education teacher would be (1) self-controlled relaxation skills, (2) cognitive restructuring, (3) participant modeling, (4) assertiveness training, and (5) coping-skills training. For example, in *relaxation training* the individual is taught to relax each muscle group in the body until the entire body is relaxed. The individual is instructed to remain relaxed while imagining stressful situations in increasing severity, until he or she can maintain optimal relaxation while imagining the most stressful situation (*systematic desensitization*). In *assertiveness training*, individuals express their own wishes without infringing on the rights of others.

In the previous example, Miss Jones may ultimately need to confront the principal in order to develop support for the use of teaching strategies that make noise and allow for physical movement among students. But, if she finds the very idea of asking the principal for a new room or explaining why her students are noisy to be stressful, relaxation training and assertiveness training can prepare her to do so.

Teachers can use other coping techniques in the management of stress as well. *Environmental planning* is merely a readjustment of the individual's life and environment to avoid the stress-provoking stimulus. For the individual who finds that working with a certain type of exceptional child is stressful, it would mean changing to working with another type. Or the teacher whose classroom activities are arranged in such a way that they cause undue amounts of stress may need to reorganize these in a different manner. *Relabeling* is essentially renaming a negatively perceived experience as a positive one. The special education teacher who is called in by the principal frequently to discuss teaching duties may find this a stressful experience. Relabeling it from a negative to a positive experience may mean that the teacher redefines the meeting as an opportunity to display his or her extensive knowledge of the field and to use the time to lobby for additional materials. For example, Mr. Ruiz, a speech pathologist who has been called in by the principal because he was heard frequently using incorrect grammar when talking to his students, can use this opportunity to present his knowledge of Black English, how it systematically differs from standard English, and strategies for teaching students to code-switch.

Self-talk is subvocal communication with oneself about the worst-case scenario outcome of an event. According to this, the teacher should begin to realize that the perceived importance and impact of the event may not be all that extensive. *Thought stopping* is a process of interrupting negative thinking, invoking the relaxation response, and then substituting a positive thought. A teacher who, when approaching the classroom for the start of the school day, finds himself or herself thinking "I can't go through another day in there" can use thought stopping by saying: "Stop!" then taking a deep breath to relax, and then thinking: "I can do this. I am good at this. I look forward to doing this."

Many special education teachers of minority students believe they have been adequately prepared and that they are competent, but that the real difficulty lies in dealing with the administrators' lack of understanding. A teacher can usually manage the stress that results from such situations appropriately through assertive behaviors.

Consider the following situation:

The principal appears at the door of the learning disability classroom with a student in tow.

"Ms. Miller, would you please keep Laura in your room for the

158

rest of the day? She is having a difficult day, and she fits in well with the kids in your room. Besides, you only have six kids in here."

"Sure, Ms. Kent. Bring her right in, there is plenty of room."

But in the teacher's mind another conversation is going on: "I don't believe the insensitive, ignorant attitudes. She doesn't realize I have six kids because I do individualized teaching to learning disabled children. And besides, by her reference to fitting in well with the kids in here, she is obviously referring to the fact that most of the kids in my room are Black and because Laura is Black it is the best place for her. I know I am going to have to spend most of my time with Laura whom everyone knows has behavior problems."

According to the assertiveness model, the teacher showed nonassertive behavior in that she denied her own wishes to satisfy someone else's. The appropriate assertive response would have been one in which she expressed her own wishes politely, feeling good about having done so, while not infringing on the rights of others. Assertive behavior becomes especially important here because nonassertiveness may result in denying racial and ethnic minority special-education children their right to fair and equal education. Consider that in the above scenario, the learning disabled students are not receiving their rightful share of the classroom instruction when Ms. Miller allows another student to be "dumped" in her room.

A major source of stress that special education teachers report is the huge of amount of paperwork required of them. Stress management involves good time management. Time management includes the following: (1) assessing how you are spending time, (2) setting goals, (3) prioritizing, (4) scheduling, (5) maximizing your rewards, (6) saying no, (7) delegating, (8) evaluating tasks once, (9) using a circular file, and (10) limiting interruptions.

Managing stress does not necessarily change the problems teachers encounter, but it helps them maintain the energy and drive to confront problems. Burnt-out teachers cannot serve their own students effectively, much less press for changes in how the school, the administration, or other teachers deal with students. In the next section we discuss strategies for confronting injustices in the school. Confrontation can bring about more stress if teachers have not learned to manage it. Thus, we see personal stress management and collective work for change as interlocking strategies that special education teachers can use to address persistent equity issues in schools.

WORKING COLLECTIVELY FOR CHANGE

Many unfair institutional processes could be changed if sufficient pressure were put on school systems to do so. Conceivably, specialists could act as a powerful source of pressure if they were to work collectively. However, most teachers do not see themselves as political activists, nor do most know much about how to consolidate and use their collective power to change schools. Patricia Ashton and Rodman Webb (1986) discussed the powerlessness teachers feel when they have "reified what they call 'the system' "(p. 51).

As part of a study of teachers in a multicultural education staff-development program, one of us (Sleeter 1991) asked 16 teachers how much power they believed the program's participants had to change the schools. Most of their responses suggested that they had never thought about this. Two simply said they had no idea. Half of them defined such change as talking with other teachers in an effort to change their attitudes. They perceived the individual teacher as the unit of change, and persuasion and enlightenment as the main change strategies. They were not very optimistic, however, about their power to change the attitudes of many teachers. One said:

160

> The people that we want to reach and that we would like to change are not going to change. . . . I know from statements that have been made to me by teachers here, that a lot of them feel that it is a waste of time. You know, a lot of our teachers are simply not going to change because they would have to get new material.

Two teachers described attitude change as requiring a sales strategy. Two expressed concern that they as teachers do not have time in their workday to concentrate on changing their colleagues' attitudes, and they would need release time in order to do so. A few teachers focused their comments on changing their own classrooms, believing that if they could make an impact on their students, broader changes would eventually occur.

Only two teachers discussed organizing to press collectively for changes. For example, one of the special education teachers said:

> I think the only way there can be any impact is if teachers identify goals—a couple of goals that everybody is going to work on, everybody is going to lobby for. . . what are the most urgent needs in this school district. Everybody would petition, hassle, coerce, cajole their building principal into recognizing these needs and trying to do something about them.

While neither of the two teachers developed her ideas about collective action and pressure politics any further, both did recognize a need for institutional changes and collective work to bring about such changes.

Those of you who recognize many of the problems related to multiculturalism and special education may be feeling quite powerless because you are only one person. But teachers can act powerfully if they act together; the teaching profession has quite a history of teacher activism and collective work for change. The suggestions that follow have been drawn from the work of Lee Staples, a well-seasoned community organizer

(Staples 1984); we think teachers can borrow very profitably from them.

First, identify your allies. Relabel yourself from being one lone person to being part of a fairly large constituency. Your constituency consists of people with common interests and concerns: low-income and racial- or language-minority families and families with children who for various reasons are not succeeding in school. Others include special education teachers and administrators who believe "the system" is not fair, general education teachers who agree with you (there are some, particularly many teachers of color), and students whom general education is failing. Collectively, their main concern is to get schools to respond more constructively to children.

Next, conceptualize your work in long-range rather than short-range terms. Your main long-range goal is to shift the balance of power in favor of those who are currently relatively powerless within the education system and community. You will face short-term issues, such as which intelligence assessment procedures to use, how to use parent input in team meetings, and so forth. Pick and choose your issues and the strategies you use so that you involve an increasing number of people, gradually winning increasingly large issues. The better organized and more involved the whole constituency becomes, the more successes it will have, and after a while, the less you will feel as though you are doing everything to effect a particular outcome on a particular issue.

For example, assume you are working in a school in which language-minority students, especially those from low-income homes, are routinely dumped in special education. A few people grumble about it, but nobody is doing anything. There are probably many problems and unmet needs that relate directly to this one problem, such as a lack of bilingual programming, low expectations of language-minority and low-income students, and poor home-school relations. Ultimately, the most mileage will result if an active coalition develops that involves teachers, sympathetic general-education teachers and administrators, and community leaders. You can begin to mobilize this constituency by starting with one issue they can probably win, such as insisting that all referrals to special education be fully explained to parents in their native language and that all communication with the school be done bilingually (which is legally their right, anyway). Once this issue is won, move on to a more difficult one.

The group collectively will press for certain key changes, and they need to be those that the constituency recognizes as important. To identify them, find people who already serve as leaders for the various constituent groups and listen to them. This may sound a bit overwhelming, but some of these people very well may be parents of students in your class and are therefore quite accessible. For example, you and other special education teachers may feel that lack of aides in your classroom is an important issue, but parents may be more concerned about unfair discipline procedures used in the school. They will be much more likely to support you in challenging the discipline procedures than in getting more aides, at least at first. Once you help work on an issue they see as important, they will be more likely to work with you on an issue you deem important.

In addition, find out if there are existing organizations that would assist you. For example, Black churches are often very concerned about Black children's achievement in school and would help organize people and press for changes in the schools if they agreed with you on the same problems and issues.

As you plan how to address an issue, examine the power structure in which it is embedded: Who benefits from current practices? Who has legitimate decision-making power? What concerns drive most of their decisions? (For example, is cost the main consideration the school board applies to most of its decisions?) What kinds of pressure tactics have other groups used with some success? What kinds of pressure tactics have failed miserably? These are the sorts of questions that can help you identify strategies that may be successful.

CONCLUSION

We wish we could say that schools are improving all the time, that teachers do not need to get involved in anything except teaching, and that the rewards of teaching will far outweigh the stress. We wish we could report that students of color and language-minority students are no longer placed disproportionately in special education, while white students are classified disproportionately as gifted; that assessment procedures are no longer biased; and that the placement process is fair to everyone. We wish we could report that schools are becoming increasingly fair places for all students. But we cannot.

What we have tried to do, however, is provide some direction for teachers who will find themselves facing issues of fairness in their own teaching. We focused particularly on special education teachers, who, by virtue of the fact that they teach students served least well by the rest of the school, will confront such problems often. These issues will probably cause you stress. We urge you to plan for that and develop strategies to manage stress so you can continue to serve students effectively. You must develop networks with others who are facing similar equity issues and practice working together to confront them. Using this approach, you can create a school that serves all of its students and its community well.

REFERENCES

Ashton, P. and Webb, R. 1986. *Making a difference: Teachers' sense of efficacy and student achievement.* New York: Longman Publishers.

Cummins, J. 1988. A theoretical framework for bilingual special education. *Exceptional Children* 54 (4): 320.

Duran, R.P. 1989. Assessment and instruction of at-risk Hispanic students. *Exceptional Children* 56 (2):154–59.

Ellis, A. and Harper, R. 1975. *A new guide to rational living.* North Hollywood, Calif.: Melvin Powers, Wilshire Book Co.

Lynch, E.W. and Lewis, R.B. 1983. Multicultural considerations in assessment and treatment of learning disabilities. *Learning Disabilities:*

An Interdisciplinary Journal 1 (8): 93–103.

Macmillan, D.L.; Hendrick, I.G.; and Watkins, A.V. 1988. Impact of Diana, Larry P. and PL 94–142 on minority students. *Exceptional Children* 54 (5): 427.

Maheady, L. et al. 1984. Minority overrepresentation in special education: A functional assessment perspective. *Special Services in the Schools* 1 (2): 5–19.

Meichenbaum, D. 1972. Cognitive modification of test anxious students. *Journal of Counseling and Clinical Psychology* 39: 370–380.

Ortiz, A.A. and Maldonado-Colon, E. 1986. Recognizing learning disabilities in bilingual children. *Journal of Reading, Writing, and Learning Disabilities International* 2 (1): 43–56.

Reschly, D.J. 1988. Minority MMR overrepresentation and special education reform. *Exceptional Children* 54 (4): 320.

Selye, H. 1956. *The stress of life.* New York: McGraw-Hill Book Co.

Sleeter, C. 1992. *Keepers of the American dream.* London, England: Falmer Press.

Smith, G.R. 1983. Desegregation and assignment to classes for the mildly retarded and learning disabled. *Integrated Education* 21: 208–11.

Staples, L. 1984. *Roots to power: A manual for grassroots organizing.* New York: Praeger.

Stern, J.D. ed. 1987. *The condition of education.* Washington, DC: U.S. Government Printing Office.

Tucker, J.A. 1980. Ethnic proportions in classes for the learning disabled: Issues in nonbiased assessment. *Journal of Special Education* 14: 93–105.

Wolpe, J. 1973. *The practice of behavior therapy.* 2nd ed. New York: Pergamon Press.

Chapter 11

EDUCATING FOR HUMAN RIGHTS: A CURRICULAR BLUEPRINT

by Ricardo L. Garcia

Education for human rights is an approach that strives to teach universal ethics about human dignity. It teaches students to respect the rights of individuals so that they can better practice their own rights (the first steps toward moral competence and social responsibility). The ethics of human rights attempt to transcend the values and norms of all societies and cultures with the intent of allowing people to practice their own cultures without violating the rights of others with whom they may or may not share cultures.

You could say that the ethics of human rights are ideal constructs of justice: They are ethics that attempt to define the social conditions necessary for all people to experience dignity throughout their lives. The human-rights approach is based on a philosophy of human interdependence, or on the idea that the fates of all humans are linked. Much like the line of John Donne's poem: "No man is an island, entire to itself," the human-rights approach operates on the belief that all humans are members of one community—the human community—so that their individual fates are inextricably linked to the fates of others.

The Universal Declaration of Human Rights issued in 1948 by the General Assembly of the United Nations included this statement about human rights:

> recognition of the inherent dignity and of the equal and inalienable rights of all members of the human family is the foundation of freedom, justice, and peace in the world.

This declaration boldly asserted the faith that peace was possible if all people would commit themselves to human rights, if all humans regardless of their affiliation with groups—race, religion, nation, social class, gender, ethnic group, tribe—would commit themselves to the belief that people as individuals are entitled to a dignified life.

The Universal Declaration of Human Rights was issued as people were moving from a world at war to a world at peace. The hope was that humanity had learned that war has no winners. All are losers, and among them the noncombatants and the innocent often suffer the most. The categorical imperative of the postwar era was "we had better learn to live together in peace, or we shall destroy each other in war." Four decades later, as we contemplate the onset of the twenty-first century, that mandate may still be true. The traditional enemies of all people—ignorance, poverty, hunger, war, disease—like the Four Horsemen of the Apocalypse, still run rampant across the land. But, we have become better at fighting some of these enemies.

During the past four decades, we have become more effective at waging war. We have even developed weapons that will kill people in their homes without damaging their houses. Without the inconvenience of rebuilding structures, conquerors can move into the undamaged houses of the vanquished. But even barring the windows will not protect these "victors" from the nuclear rain and winds that another aggressor can use to annihilate the plants and animals that serve as food for all the combatants.

We are better at waging war against disease. We have developed "wonder" drugs, vaccines, and preventative medicines that ameliorate suffering and pain, thereby extending the quality and quantity of life. Is it progress, then, to claim that we have achieved parity at both saving and killing life? I would argue that we are better at killing than at saving life, although we have attained high levels of technical competence in both areas.

How do we make use of our high level of technical competence? We have centuries of experience with teaching people to save and to kill life. We have less experience with teaching that helps people understand how to use knowledge in a socially responsible manner, especially in a pluralistic world that is growing interdependent. We need to rise to a new plateau of competence, to a level of moral proficiency where we use our newfound knowledge to improve the conditions of life and learn to live together in peace. Schools and teachers cannot achieve this ideal alone. What they can do is seek to improve the relationships within their own classrooms by creating a belief that we are all interdependent members of the human community.

SCHOOLING AS A COMMUNITY AFFAIR

The genius of schools throughout the United States is that they are embedded in communities. In a larger sense, they are embedded in a variety of communities and are affected by what happens within their respective states, the country as a whole, and of course, the world. What these variegated communities have in common are people, human beings who collectively form a human community.

The human community consists of billions of people who speak different languages and practice different cultures. While vast differences in ideologies, religions, and values attest to the human community's plurality, all the people share an interdependence of fates. We all live on the same planet, breathe the same air, and drink the same water. The storage of toxic wastes in the desert of New Mexico, the destruction of the rain forests of Brazil, and the precipitation of acid rain in highly industrialized regions of Europe all affect the air we breathe and the water we drink, regardless of where we live.

For better or worse, schools and teachers play a role in shaping the human community. Schools and teachers are legally mandated to transmit the basic skills and knowledge of academic disciplines—language, mathematics, science, social studies, physical and health education, and the arts, or what I earlier referred to as technical competence. Furthermore, they are morally challenged to prepare their students to live within the broader human community as socially responsible citizens; therefore, they also teach moral competence. While schools will reflect the prevailing values and cultures of their local communities, and while transmission of the basic skills and knowledge of academic disciplines may prepare students to live within their local communities, the schools and their teachers are challenged to prepare their students to live in a pluralistic, globally interdependent human community. Schools should not be mirrors that reflect the values and beliefs of their local communities; rather, they should be windows to the world that exists beyond their own community.

The global challenge places schools and teachers in the position of responding to political, economic, religious, and social forces that exist outside the school's neighborhood, while concurrently responding to the values and aspirations of the people within the local community. Teachers can work toward the goal of creating socially responsible humans by construing the educational experience as a social contract entered into by students and teachers in which human rights play a central role in the day-to-day classroom routine.

RIGHTS AS FUNDAMENTAL PRINCIPLES

Rights are not merely high-sounding ideals. Rights are fundamental principles that people can use to guide their relationships with other people. They are social in character and exist within a socially interactive context. Therefore, rights function within the context of a group or community and prescribe the behavioral parameters allowed individuals within it.

Rights define the kind and degree of freedom individuals are allowed within their societies. Too much or too little freedom would be destructive to a human group. Too much freedom would create chaos and disorder; too little freedom would stifle creativity and stymie group development. Within any group or community, there exists a need to balance the rights (freedoms) of the individual with the rights of all the people in the group. Rights as social-interaction entitlements allow individuals to act

169

as free agents within the parameters established by their group or community. As such, rights are correlative: For every right given to the individual within a society, there exists a concurrent responsibility that the individual owes all the members of the society, that is, respect for the rights of others.

There are important differences between the kind of rights that people enjoy. *Civil rights* are granted to individuals by their governments and are supposed to protect the individual from the arbitrary behavior of the state's leaders. The twelfth-century charter of Henry I and the thirteenth-century charter of King John (the Magna Carta) were agreements between the king and his barons. The charters stated the rights of the king and the barons, which served to limit the power of the king. The principle that laws should limit the power of governments and protect the individual from the arbitrary behavior of government officials emerged from these charters. In the nineteenth century, the Bill of Rights was added to the United States Constitution to specify the rights vested in citizens, protecting them from the arbitrary behavior of those in power.

The potency of civil rights lies within the power of the laws behind them. However, civil rights are only as good as the people who enforce them. For example, even though the Thirteenth Amendment freed all African American slaves, thereby granting them civil rights, Jim Crow laws were enacted that effectively blocked African Americans from practicing their civil rights. How did this happen? It happened because officials failed to enforce the civil rights granted to African Americans by the Thirteenth Amendment to the United States Constitution.

Cultural rights refer to the prerogatives of group membership. For example, as a member of a certain cultural group, individuals are entitled to a sense of community and historical connectedness. In other words, individuals within the group are linked by common traditions, customs, and symbols that provide them with a feeling of belonging to a group, which in turn, forges a self-identity for the individuals. Further, the individuals are entitled to the knowledge that they are linked to a long history of events and people, thereby preventing social alienation.

To maintain the group's prerogatives, its members conceive certain behaviors as appropriate or inappropriate for the security or perpetuation of the group. Cultural rights are focused on the group's need to maintain conformity and order within it. Cultural rights protect the group from the arbitrary behavior of individual members. Cultural rights have the power of customs and traditions to enforce them. Minimal deviations from the group's norms are accepted; extreme deviations are punished through banishment or ostracism. If individuals wish to remain within the group and receive its protection and security, then they must conform to the group's norms. In other words, individuals are free to accept or reject a group's norms.

Civil and cultural rights are limited in their scope. They exist within the context of a given province, such as a nation or an ethnic group. Protection of civil rights varies over time and with different groups. Cultural rights are limited to members of a particular group, thereby depriving nonmembers of rights gained by group membership or conformity to its norms.

Human rights, on the other hand, are universal in scope. They apply to all humans in all parts of the world. They transcend the provinciality of civil and cultural rights, but they do not exist in legally formulated constitutions or governments, nor do they necessarily exist within historically established ethnic or cultural groups. Consequently, human rights do not have the legal power of civil rights or the coercive power of cultural rights. Human rights exist as constructs of perfect justice emphasizing what people hold in common in a globally interdependent society or community.

THE ROOTS OF HUMAN RIGHTS

Human rights are based on a philosophy of human dignity and consist of a cluster of ethics regarding individuals and their relationship with others. They operate on the faith that human relationships can be governed by ethics that transcend all cultural differences.

Ancient Greek philosophers believed that the world was organized in a balanced, harmonious order. Humans, as a part of the natural order of things in nature, were ultimately controlled by laws held in common by all humankind. The greatest virtue was to know the natural law and live in conformity with it, that is, the greatest virtue was to live in harmony with humans in a group. The Ancient Greeks perceived individuals as "corporate persons" whose duty was to join a group (ethnic group, religion, nation, tribe) and then pursue its interests. In short, people existed for groups. During the latter decades of the European Middle Ages, scholars shifted the focus from people as corporate persons to people as individuals. As individuals, people were free to join or not join groups. Scholars such as John Locke, Jean J. Rosseau, and Adam Smith stressed the individual nature of social interaction. Smith, for example, argued that if individuals were allowed to pursue their own self-interests without mercantile interference, then both the individual and the nation could prosper. This was the basic thesis of Smith's classic text, *The Wealth of Nations*. The English philosopher Locke (1947)is credited for formulating the philosophy of political individualism and freedom. In his text, *On Civil Government*, published in 1689, he postulated:

> The state of nature has a law to govern it. . .reason, which. . .teaches all mankind. . .being all equal and independent, no one ought to harm another in his life, health, liberty, or possessions.

Thomas Jefferson placed Locke's notion of individual rights and freedoms in the Declaration of Independence.

Human rights germinated as a consequence of the union between the Ancient Greek notion of the natural order of all things and the European worldview of people as individuals entitled to freedom of action within the natural order. Human rights are based on the following *a priori* assumptions:

- *All humans are members of one race, the human race.* Humans may differ intellectually and physically, but these differences are subordinate to the fundamental humanity shared by all people. In other words, being human takes precedence over physical or intellectual differences.
- *Humans exist as ends in themselves.* Individuals are not born to serve masters, although they are free to submit their fates to a master, such as a government, a teacher, or a God.
- *Humans are ethically equal.* The belief in human rights acknowledges the existence of intellectual, economic, political, and physical inequalities. Yet, the existence of these inequalities do not justify ethical treatment that is inequitable.
- *Humans live in communities governed by natural law and civil law.* All people live within a civil society and a human society. The civil society consists of the individual's state, province, or nation in which citizenship is held. The human society is the totality of all humanity. There are no national boundaries to the human society. Rather, the society is governed by those rights that dignify individual humans, or what Locke called the "law of nature."
- *Within the human society, for every right there exists a concurrent responsibility.* If all humans are to have equal treatment or rights, all must respect the rights of others. Mutual respect of rights is the axle that keeps the wheel of human rights moving within the human society.

These assumptions, namely that all people as members of the human race are ends in themselves entitled to equal treatment under the law with the duty of showing respect for the rights of others, are succinctly summarized in the preamble of the Declaration of Independence:

We hold these truths to be self-evident, that all men are created equal, that they are endowed by their Creator with certain unalienable rights, that among these are Life, Liberty, and the pursuit of Happiness.

Life, liberty, and the pursuit of happiness are fundamental human rights. How can they be taught in the classroom?

HUMAN RIGHTS IN THE CLASSROOM

Human rights really cannot be taught didactically; students are more apt to practice the ethics they experience rather than the ethics they are told to embrace. In other words, human rights should be *caught* rather than *taught.*

Of course, human rights in action are hardly possible without education, or freedom from ignorance. Schools and teachers have the responsibility of educating all of their students so that they may exercise their human rights. But, teachers should work toward the goal of creating socially responsible students who are able to live in a pluralistic and globally interdependent human community by treating the classroom experience as a social contract entered into by students and teachers alike. Social responsibility can be caught by the students rather than taught in the daily interplay of the classroom as a social contract.

A social contract is an agreement among humans made to protect the rights of individuals so that they may pursue their better interests. In pursuits of interests, individuals can benefit the community and themselves. Students in a classroom that operates as a social contract enter into an agreement with their teachers and the other students to respect the rights of others while pursuing their own interests.

Pursuit of interests means learning. Consequently, the classroom is a community of scholars engaged in learning. They hold in common the overall goal of learning whatever the teacher has to offer, and while they may differ in terms of race, ethnicity, language, religion, class, gender, or physical and intellectual capabilities, they are nonetheless a community sharing an interdependence of fates. As a community, they stand or fall, depending on the quality and quantity of learning that occurs within their classroom. Individual students have a responsibility to the community to initiate activities that allow all of them to learn. They are all duty-bound to take learning into their own hands.

While pursuing learning, students should respect the rights of other students to learn. Students should be encouraged to pursue learning competitively and cooperatively so long as individual students are responsible for their own learning. There is no pedagogical justification for making all learning activities competitive. Often, students can help each other learn, as has been the experience with cooperative-learning experiments conducted by Robert Slavin and his colleagues at Johns Hopkins University in Baltimore, Maryland (Slavin, 1986). Excessive use of competitive modes lends itself to a "win-at-any-cost" learning strategy in which there are only a few winners and many losers. The approach, used excessively, is inimical for learning social responsibility. The same is true with the excessive use of a cooperative approach that might cause learning to drop to a very low common denominator.

What follows is a human-rights blueprint that incorporates the human rights of life, liberty, and the pursuit of happiness into a classroom context. The blueprint can be used as a guide for operating a classroom as a social contract intended to foster learning of academic subjects as well as social responsibility.

175

PREAMBLE: The classroom operates as a community of scholars who are engaged in learning. The individual's right to learn is protected and respected by all scholars. Scholars should initiate learning; teachers should initiate instruction, balancing the rights of individuals with the rights of other individuals in the community.

A. RIGHT TO EXIST or safe occupancy of space: The classroom is a physically safe learning environment.

- Classroom fixtures and furnishings are in good repair and otherwise nonhazardous.
- Classroom is well ventilated and well lighted, and the temperature is comfortable.
- Teacher does not allow students to physically harm each other.
- Teacher does not allow throwing of objects or other risky behavior that endangers students.

B. RIGHT TO LIBERTY or freedom of conscience and expression.

- Teacher allows students to assert their opinions.
- Teacher fosters respectful student dissension as a means for rational understanding of issues and divergent opinions.
- Teacher enforces dress and hairstyle codes that allow for individual and group differences.
- Teacher fosters examination of each student's ethnic or cultural heritage. Teachers should help students become "ethnically literate" about their own individual cultural backgrounds as well as the backgrounds of others.

C. RIGHT TO HAPPINESS or self-esteem: The classroom is a safe, emotional learning environment that fosters self-esteem among the students.

- Teacher does not tease, ridicule, or demean students.
- Teacher does not foster name-calling; elitist, racist, or sexist slurs; or stereotypical expressions in the classroom.
- Teacher does not reveal confidential documents, term papers, or notes to the whole class without the permission of the author.
- Teacher does not reveal grades or remarks on class projects or term papers to the whole class without permission of the student.
- Teacher disciplines students equally, insuring that minority students are not punished more severely than majority group students for the same infractions.
- f linguistic and cultural respect by using linguistically and culturally relevant curriculum materials and instructional strategies, telling the students that their language and culture are welcome in the classroom community.

CONCLUSION

During the 1970s, the human-rights approach emerged out of concern for the rights of minorities. The truth was, students were being denied fundamental civil rights in schools and classrooms. In 1976, Phi Delta Kappa, the professional educational organization, issued a Human Rights Creed in Education, which pledged that teachers and schools would guard the civil rights of students.

While the human-rights approach still can serve its earlier purpose, human-rights instruction for the twenty-first century requires teachers to prepare students to act as socially responsible individuals within a pluralistic, globally interdependent human community. Socially responsible individuals require more than technical competence; they need the ability to function with diverse peoples, cultures, and languages. They need to be morally competent individuals who are able to transcend cultural differences without denigrating or ignoring the differences.

The human-rights approach evolved as a means by which students can be taught fundamental ethical principles to govern all of their human relationships. The approach requires schools and teachers to conduct their classrooms as a community of scholars in pursuit of learning. Students are encouraged to take responsibility for their own learning; teachers, as leaders of the classroom community, help students enter a social contract in which everyone has rights and concurrent responsibilities to respect the rights of others. As disputes and differences of opinion emerge, the teacher guides the students through negotiations that help them develop skills in conflict resolution without recourse to violence. The ultimate hope is that if students can learn to resolve differences peacefully in their classrooms, then they will have the moral competence to resolve differences peacefully within the broader human community.

REFERENCES

Locke, J. *On Civil Government: The second treatise.* Chicago: Great Books Press, 1947.

Slavin, R.E. 1986. *Using student team learning.* 3rd ed. Baltimore, Md: Center for Research on Elementary and Middle Schools, the Johns Hopkins University.

Universal Declaration of Human Rights. 1948. New York: The United Nations. Document can be copied for educational purposes. Or, contact Netherlands Commission for UNESCO, Oranjestraat 10, 2514 JB The Hague, The Netherlands.

Chapter 12

INSTITUTIONALIZING MULTI-CULTURAL EDUCATION IN TEACHER EDUCATION PROGRAMS

by Norene F. Daly and Deborah J. O'Dowd

Throughout its short history, the United States has demanded assimilation of "mainstream values" from all who reached its shores. Public schools were established to be the vehicles of this national cohesion, vehicles that promoted a republican government and served the needs of industry. More specifically, schools were expected to teach academic subjects and conformity to social norms. Educators have been agents of assimilation and control as well as facilitators of change and emancipation. Countless children have benefited from education's promise of a better future; however, our country continues to deny societal benefits to vast numbers of Americans based on characteristics as arbitrary as ethnicity, gender, and/or class.

THE MYTH OF THE MELTING POT

One need only consider the characteristics of the United States to begin to understand the pluralism that exists within its borders. America is a vast land whose citizens come from the farthest reaches of the globe and represent every major racial and religious group. Its citizens range from the very richest to the very poorest; both young and old; both able-bodied and physically challenged. Total assimilation has been avoided by all who endeavored to protect their cultural identity. Those who have resisted the notion of sacrificing their culture and traditions argue that the exigency for them to do so is in direct conflict with the ideals of equality and justice. It also has become apparent that the call for assimilation has worked against the educational attainment of generations of children. The schools have been guilty of segregation, the denigration of immigrant children, and the placement of a disproportionate number of language- and cultural-minority children in special education classes (McCormick 1984).

In the early 1900s, educators and philosophers began to question the validity of the melting-pot myth, and an increasing number of writers argued for the promotion and preservation of ethnic-group identity. In 1924, Horace Kallen coined the term *cultural pluralism* to describe the United States. Cultural pluralism is generally understood as:

> a societal condition in which members of ethnic groups may choose to practice a great deal or a little of their ethnic heritage without fear of political or physical reprisal, in which different cultural values, beliefs, and behaviors are accepted, and in which different ethnic communities are allowed to exist side-by-side. (Condianni and Tipple 1980)

The seeds for ethnic studies were planted in the 1930s. Organizations, such as the Service Bureau for Intercultural Education, were founded to promote the acceptance of, and respect for, the differences students brought to the classroom and to look for ways to eliminate discrimination. Educators began to suggest that the majority population could be made more tolerant of new immigrants through the use of intercultural and ethnic studies. This alternative, though not popularly accepted, found immediate support from religious groups, the American Council on Education (ACE), the Anti-Defamation League, and the National Education Association (NEA). In 1945, a consortium was formed to conduct research and develop a philosophy of intergroup education. The consortium sponsored the Intergroup Education in Cooperating Schools project, which enjoyed the support of ACE and the National Conference of Christians and Jews. In addition to this project, ACE also began the "College Study in Intergroup Relations," which was co-sponsored by the Council on Cooperation in Teacher Education. Council members included the American Association of Colleges for Teacher Education, and NEA, among others (Banks 1979).

THE BEGINNING OF INTERGROUP EDUCATION

Recognizing the impact teachers have on the formation of attitudes and assuming that schools could be influential in the establishment of positive human relations, ACE founded the Committee on the Study of Teaching Materials in Intergroup Relations in 1948. The committee recommended direct contact and interaction among members of culturally different groups as the best way to overcome stereotypes and accept diversity. Some texts were rewritten to reflect an international perspective; however, these materials were meant to supplement firsthand experiences. Issue-oriented subject matter came into vogue, and the importance of the involvement of the entire school, from administrators to students, and from curriculum and guidance to teaching methods, was stressed (Gollnick 1990).

Although time and effort were devoted to the subject, intergroup educational reforms failed to become institutionalized. James Banks (1979) theorized that the movement faded because mainstream educators neither internalized the ideology nor understood how the movement contributed to the major goals of American schools. Intergroup education was viewed as necessary only for schools that suffered open racial conflict, which during the 1950s was becoming more subtle. Additionally, the United States was a segregated country and efforts toward eliminating prejudice and discrimination were stifled by the policy of separation. Schools were among the institutions that acted as obstacles to the realization of equal rights by maintaining separate educational facilities. It was not until the 1954 *Brown v. Topeka Board of Education* decision that the American system of apartheid began to be dismantled.

The *Brown* decision gave impetus to a growing movement of ethnic pride. New leaders, such as Dorothy Height, C.T.

Vivian, and Martin Luther King, Jr., emerged and guided the populace toward expanded human rights. The Civil Rights Act of 1964, the Bilingual Education Act of 1967, and the Equal Education Act of 1974 were passed as a result of the civil-rights movement. The purpose of this legislation was to ensure that no state deny equal opportunity to any person on the basis of race, color, sex, or national origin. Departments of education in several states responded to the new laws by requiring that multicultural concepts be infused into texts and materials (Condianni and Tipple 1980). Improved intercultural relations began to re-emerge as an important educational task.

Universities, and later public schools, expanded their course offerings to include a variety of ethnic-studies classes. In general, these classes were historical, chronological, and focused on heroes of the specific ethnic group being studied. The main objectives of the classes were to acquaint the participants with their roots and increase self-esteem through ethnic pride. In 1974, Congress authorized three million dollars to fund ethnic-heritage projects. The United States Office of Education received more than 1,000 applications from several states during the first year of the program. Of these, 42 projects were funded, a number of them in colleges of education that used the funds to develop multicultural, nonsexist curricula for the preparation of teachers and for faculty development.

Throughout its short existence, the Ethnic Heritage Project Branch funded proposals concerned with curriculum and development; although prior to the elimination of the program in 1981, a large percentage of the available money was disseminated. The demand for ethnic-heritage materials still exists, and a few organizations, such as the Center for Quality Integrated Education and the NEA, continue to develop related materials, but government interest in diversity and the promotion thereof was not a high priority during the decade of the 1980s.

For the most part, schools did not embrace ethnic studies as an integral part of the curriculum. Courses in ethnic studies were usually listed as electives, and students of color enrolled in classes that matched their ethnic background. It soon became apparent that intercultural relations would not improve until members of the dominant culture learned about the contributions and accomplishments of minority groups, and minority groups learned about each other. In addition, educators began to realize that ethnic-studies programs did not result in major academic gains for minority students, and that significant improvement in achievement was only possible as a result of total school reform. It also became apparent that, with new waves of immigrants coming to America, and the growth of cultural groups in public elementary and secondary schools, there was increased demand for recognition of cultural values, preservation of native languages, and greater understanding of the contributions that the various cultures could make to an increasingly pluralistic society.

FROM ETHNIC STUDIES TO MULTICULTURAL, NONSEXIST EDUCATION

The United States was in its adolescence in the 1960s. It was a transitional era characterized by numerous and complicated issues, particularly the need to adapt to political and social change. Many citizens were engaged in a process of identity formation; re-examining old values, attitudes, and beliefs; experimenting with new ones; and calling for socially responsible behavior. Multiethnic studies mirrored this popular movement, and educators developed a theoretical framework that examined the roots of prejudice and identified institutional racism as an obstacle to equality. It was, therefore, essential to stop blaming the victims of discrimination for their lack of power and socioeconomic success, the source of which had been generally attributed to inherited or cultural characteristics (Banks 1988). In addition, women and individuals with disabilities began to recognize themselves as oppressed groups and demanded inclusion in the educational reforms that were taking place.

Multicultural, nonsexist education was born of ethnic and feminist revitalization and can be defined as instruction that provides equal opportunities for all students. It promotes effective interpersonal and intergroup relations by teaching students the historical and contemporary contributions of *all* citizens, and it demonstrates that the variety of roles open to men and women should not be limited by cultural, linguistic, ethnic, or handicapping conditions.

If real change were to occur in the nation's schools, it was obvious that teacher-preparation institutions would have to assume a leadership role in developing programs that would enable prospective teachers to become sensitive to issues of multicultural, nonsexist education in the classroom. In addition, those same institutions would have to provide in-service training for teachers who were in multicultural environments in order to provide them with knowledge of techniques and attitudes necessary to ensure that the diversity represented in their classrooms was preserved and enhanced.

THE ROLE OF NATIONAL ASSOCIATIONS

In 1969, the American Association of Colleges for Teacher Education (AACTE) published *Teachers for the Real World*, which underscored the need for more effective preparation of teachers in order to build upon cultural diversity. In 1973, AACTE again emphasized the need to restructure teacher preparation when its Commission on Multicultural Education issued *No One Model American* (AACTE 1973). This document provided a substantive rationale for the infusion of multicultural, nonsexist educational concepts in teacher-education programs:

Multicultural-education programs for teachers are more than special courses or special learning experiences grafted onto the standard program. The commitment to cultural pluralism must permeate all areas of the educational experiences provided for prospective teachers. (p. 4)

184

AACTE continued the work of informing teacher educators who would in turn prepare teachers for the very important task of recognizing and building upon the rich mix of cultures that was evident in schools. In 1974, when many institutions were developing competency-based teacher education programs, and states were beginning to require that institutions preparing teachers recognize the importance of the development of competencies for the multicultural classroom, AACTE published *Multicultural Education Through Competency-Based Teacher Education*. This publication was probably more influential than any others available at the time in affecting the initial institutionalization of multicultural, nonsexist education in teacher education.

AACTE's contribution to the knowledge base in multicultural, nonsexist education was significantly enhanced during the late 1970s and 1980s through the continuing work of its Commission on Multicultural Education and the adoption of a series of resolutions by its member institutions. The resolutions underscored the critical nature of efforts to ensure infusion of multicultural, nonsexist content throughout the teacher-education curriculum and addressed equally critical issues associated with the inclusion of minorities as faculty members within teacher-preparation institutions and the need to recruit minority students as prospective teachers.

In addition to the work of its commissions and the development of resolutions, AACTE, as a major partner in the National Council for Accreditation of Teacher Education (NCATE), was collaborating with other NCATE constituent organizations, such as the NEA and a variety of other professional associations, to revise standards for the accreditation of teacher-preparation programs. In 1977, NCATE published the first standard on multicultural education (NCATE 1977), which became effective in 1979, thereby requiring that institutions provide evidence that the infusion of multicultural, nonsexist principles had become a reality in their preparation programs, field experiences, faculty-employment practices, student recruitment, institutional governance, and governance of the professional-education unit.

The 1977 NCATE standard, which was to become the forerunner for a series of standards developed in the 1980s, built upon and reinforced the earlier efforts of AACTE to ensure the institutionalization of multicultural, nonsexist education. The preamble to the standard included the goals and definition of multicultural education and required that:

Provision should be made for instruction in multicultural education in teacher-education programs. Multicultural education should receive attention in courses, seminars, directed reading, laboratory and clinical experiences, practicum, and other types of field experiences.

The experiences recommended for multicultural education were broad and included activities that would promote the analytical problem-solving skills needed to confront issues such as racism, sexism, the unequal distribution of power, values clarification, and the dynamics of culture and language as they impact teaching strategies. Also stressed were the recognition of different learning styles and the need to develop a variety of appropriate teaching styles.

In addition to the standard, institutions were guided by a series of "evidence questions" that had been developed by AACTE's Commission on Multicultural Education in 1980. These questions required programs being reviewed by NCATE to reflect an array of issues that affected all components of the teacher-preparation program and the institutional framework wherein the program functioned. When used in conjunction with the standard, these questions proved effective in helping teacher educators develop curricula and design practical experiences that would prepare students for the realities of the classroom, especially in urban settings.

During the decade of the 1980s, NCATE undertook an extensive process that resulted in the redesign of its standards for accreditation (NCATE 1987). As part of that redesign process, 18 standards and 94 criteria for compliance were developed. Multicultural, nonsexist concepts for teacher education were specified in four of the standards and seven of the compliance criteria. In addition, NCATE issued a definition of *multicultural perspective* that was inclusive of all of the components of multicultural, nonsexist education:

> *MULTICULTURAL PERSPECTIVE*: A multicultural perspective is a recognition of (1) the social, political, and economic realities that individuals experience in culturally diverse and complex human encounters; and (2) the importance of culture, race, sex and gender, ethnicity, religion, socioeconomic status, and exceptionalities in the education process.

Teacher-education programs that reflect the plurality of the United States and the world have taken on even greater importance as school enrollment continues to reflect the growth of minority populations. AACTE and NCATE remain committed to equity education; however, they and others have encountered problems when trying to determine the extent to which multicultural, nonsexist education has been included in teacher-preparation programs throughout the country.

OBSTACLES TO INSTITUTIONALIZING MULTICULTURAL, NONSEXIST EDUCATION

The major obstacle to institutionalizing multicultural, nonsexist education seems to be definitional. What some consider multicultural, nonsexist education, others call human relations; still others use the terms interchangeably. Questions addressed to accrediting agencies and state departments of education regarding requirements for multicultural, nonsexist teacher-preparation programs are met with a series of counter-inquiries seeking clarification of terms. Some states still consider ethnic studies and multicultural, nonsexist education to be synonymous, while others claim that teacher institutions are multicultural if the characteristics of the student body are multicultural. Also, it is not always clear if multicultural, nonsexist education is merely part of an institution's elective curriculum or actually required for certification. In cases where it is required for certification, it may be required as part of the pre-service, in-service, or recertification process.

Considerations that confuse the issue even further are: the content studied, groups studied, courses offered, program length, and students and disciplines participating. To the degree that any conformity can be established, it is clear that institutions seeking NCATE accreditation must document compliance with the NCATE standards. In spite of the strong leadership shown by AACTE and NCATE, accreditation decisions since 1988 have shown that teacher education is still not multicultural (Gollnick 1990). Of the 1500 teacher-education institutions in the United States, only one-third are accredited by NCATE; the remaining programs are approved by states whose requirements may or may not include a multicultural, nonsexist education approach.

In 1990, NCATE reported the following data for the first 109 institutions reviewed under the revised multicultural standards:

	Standard	Institutions Not Meeting Standard	Institutions With Weakness Only	Combined Percent Of Total
I.A	Professional Studies	6	40	42.2%
II.A	Clinical and Field-Based Experiences	3	33	33.0%
III.A	Student Admission	12	51	57.8%
IV.A	Faculty Qualifications And Assignments	19	44	57.8%

Among the weaknesses cited in the area of multicultural experiences were:

- lack of preparation to work with exceptional students,
- lack of development of a wide array of teaching strategies to adequately meet diverse learning styles,
- lack of emphasis on content or experiences that would increase awareness and sensitivity to cultural diversity. (Gollnick 1990)

Multicultural, nonsexist education seems to be a polarizing issue that has left some educators calling for the reintroduction of an assimilationist model (Lindsay 1982) while others clamor for the need to develop a national multicultural, nonsexist education theory (Lee 1983). This philosophical division appears to be at least partially responsible for the deficiencies still found in teacher-education programs.

There is also a lack of national leadership to help educators deal with issues of diversity. In fact, multicultural, nonsexist education is viewed by the federal government as an academic problem that deals with integrating students, especially ethnic minorities, into existing systems. Although it will admit that changing demographic plurality is a major challenge, the government is not inclined to give money to issues of diversity and remains devoted to the sponsorship of one national culture (Karelis 1990).

This attitude is reflected in many educational institutions. Although the majority of institutions accredited by NCATE have recruitment plans for attracting a multicultural faculty and student body, the plans appear to be inadequate because the institutions have not been successful in recruiting or retaining the diversity that is desired.

Educators are also struggling with the question of strategies. The AACTE collected case studies from various institutions (Gollnick 1980) to present alternative strategies for implementing multicultural, nonsexist education programs.

Exemplary programs, many of which had been developed in response to community needs, had revised the core professional teacher-education courses to reflect a multicultural emphasis in human interactions; however, there are a number of approaches that are used to implement multicultural, nonsexist education.

One of the most prevalent approaches, still in use is an *add-on* approach, which is the use of the standard curriculum with multicultural issues tacked on somewhere along the line. This approach inhibits concept development, does nothing to reform the structure of the curriculum, and leaves educators with the impression that multicultural, nonsexist education is yet another task to be completed in their field or subject.

It is possible that the term *multicultural, nonsexist education* is, in itself, an obstacle to its wider acceptance. Some educators argue for more readily acceptable or contemporary terminology and offer *culturally responsive pedagogy* as a possible alternative.

A review of the literature and a survey of practitioners' views show that the reform movement has done little to promote educational equity or close the gender achievement-gap (Sadker, Sadker, and Steindam 1989). Feminism has a very negative media image. That, coupled with the fact that teaching is a female-dominated occupation, controlled in large part by the public sector, may help to explain the lack of importance paid to gender equity. The need to establish new terminology, develop concepts that permeate the curriculum, and fully integrate multicultural, nonsexist education as a vital component of teacher preparation programs is apparent.

CONCLUSION

Institutions must move beyond the add-on approach to multicultural, nonsexist education. The add-on approach leaves both educators and students with the impression that contributions made by diverse members of society are incidental to those made by the white middle class. It reinforces the feeling of superiority among the latter group and serves to increase resistance to mainstream education on the part of minority students. When students fail to see themselves positively reflected in the school curriculum, they soon become disenchanted with the educational system and drop out of school in disproportionate numbers. For many of them, inequality leads to alienation.

When historical events are presented in the classroom, it is imperative that a wide variety of perspectives are included in the lessons. The perspective of European settlers as they moved west was very different from the perspective of those indigenous to the area. If the goal is to promote critical thinking and socially responsible decision-making skills in students, historical omissions and distortions must not be tolerated.

Teacher-education programs should strive to replace the old melting-pot myth with a new "fruit-salad" model representative of the many ethnic, cultural, religious, and language groups that make up the United States. The approach used, the faculty hired, and the student body taught must reflect the demographics of the nation.

The issue of inclusion is central to any discussion of multicultural, nonsexist education. In the last 20 years, fluctuations in the economy have increased competition between groups. At the present time, it cannot be assumed that all groups are automatically included under the multicultural, nonsexist education umbrella. Those most active in the field are working to ensure that the movement continues to grow and become operational, especially in those institutions not accredited by NCATE. The interconnectedness of issues such as race, class, and gender must be continually emphasized to prevent them from being lost in a battle for scarce resources.

Teachers must be prepared to develop lesson plans that show all persons as potentially productive members of society who have the power to change and improve that society. Educational programs that expose and purge the obstacles to empowerment in the form of racism must be designed. To fail to do so is to fail the future.

REFERENCES

American Association of Colleges for Teacher Education (AACTE). 1973. No one model American. *Journal of Teacher Education* 24 (4).

Banks, J.A. 1988. *Multicultural education: Theory Into practice.* Boston: Allyn and Bacon.

Banks, J.A. 1979. Multiethnic multicultural teacher education: Conceptual, historical, and ideological issues. Paper presented at the Institute on Multiethnic Studies for Teacher Education. Dallas, Tx.

Condianni, A.V. and Tipple, B.E. 1980. Conceptual changes in ethnic studies. *Viewpoints in Teaching and Learning* 56 (1): 26–37.

Gollnick, D. 1990. Race, class and gender in teacher education. Washington, DC: National Council for Accreditation of Teacher Education. Unpublished document.

Gollnick, D. 1980. *Multicultural teacher education: Case studies of 13 programs.* Vol. II. Washington, DC: American Association of Colleges for Teacher Education.

Karelis, C. 1990. Conversation with Karelis, Director of Fund for the Improvement of Postsecondary Education, U.S. Department of Education. November 1990.

Lee, M.K. 1983. Multiculturalism: Educational perspectives for the 1980s. *Education* 103 (4): 405–9.

Lindsay, A.J. 1982. The misguided ethnic schooling of minority youth. *Journal of Teacher Education* 33 (5): 18–23.

McCormick, T. 1984. Multiculturalism: Some principles and issues. *Theory Into Practice* XXIII (2): 93–97.

National Council for Accreditation of Teacher Education. 1987. Standards, policies and procedures for the accreditation of professional education units.

National Council for Accreditation of Teacher Education. 1977. Standards for the accreditation of teacher education.

Sadker, M.; Sadker, D.; and Steindam, S. 1989. Gender equity and educational reform. *Educational Leadership* 46 (6) 44–47.

Chapter 13

RESISTANCE TO MULTICULTURAL EDUCATION: CONCERNS AND RESPONSES

by Carlos F. Díaz

As anyone who has ever tried to change curriculum knows, schools are inherently conservative institutions. The previous chapters have persuasively suggested that traditional school practices have not served many of our students well, and absent of significant change, gaps in educational achievement among students of different cultural backgrounds can be expected to remain wide or even to increase in the future.

Educators who support a multicultural curriculum and school environment must understand that their efforts will not always meet with unqualified support. There will be instances when students, parents, administrators, or teachers will react to these changes with trepidation, fear, or outright opposition. Multicultural curricular reform can generate controversy in some educational settings. This potential for controversy should not be discussed tangentially, but must be fully understood by all educators. The topics that follow are issues that represent potential obstacles to multicultural curricular change.

TEMPORARY CURRICULAR NOTION

Recently, one of my students remarked after class, "Everything you are teaching me makes sense to me, but how do I know it is not a fad?" One logical barrier to implementing multicultural education is that teachers will invest time and energy learning the multicultural dimensions of their subjects, and then emphasis in this area simply disappears. Historically, the mainstream or macrocultural perspective has dominated the

193

curriculum of American public schools. While this curricular caricature of American society has been in place for generations, the reality of American life has always been multicultural in nature.

No one can predict the cycles of future emphasis in curriculum, but teachers who develop multicultural literacy and incorporate these perspectives into their teaching can be certain that their teaching practices will be congruent with the heterogeneity present in this nation as well as in the world.

IS IT SOCIAL RECONSTRUCTIONISM?

In the 1930s, the progressive movement in American education faced a major cleavage. Works like *Dare We Build a New Social Order?* by George Counts challenged progressive educators to inculcate a particular set of values and conclusions in students. Mainstream progressives argued that progressive education should give students a wide range of information and the ability to ask probing questions, and that conclusions should be left to students themselves.

A multicultural curriculum, appropriately conceived and presented, does not attempt to force any conclusions on students. However, educators and pupils must be prepared for possible shifts in outlooks as each of them is exposed to a much broader range of information and perspectives. For instance, how might student or public opinion be affected on the issue of public-school integration if all parties had a full understanding of the case law, timetables, and enforcement practices that occurred from 1954 to the present? Most Americans have opinions, and often strong ones, on the need and mechanisms for integrating public education. Few, however, can articulate a historical perspective on this issue and base their judgment mainly on life experience. A multicultural curriculum would provide all students with a wide range of information and the analytical tools to apply that knowledge to issues like school integration and many other topics that receive cursory attention in the curriculum.

In attempting to infuse multicultural perspectives, educators should present unifying themes in society as well as circumstances that may be less flattering to our national image. The curriculum should not take the position that events be presented from the perspectives of "victims and victimizers." Likewise, topics should not be glossed over or omitted because they illustrate unequal power relationships or do not contribute to a unified notion of American society. Societal unity, in this or any other society, cannot rest on a manufactured consensus or a selective presentation of facts.

DOES MULTICULTURALISM POLITICIZE THE CURRICULUM?

A number of authors have written about potentially dangerous elements in multicultural education. Chester Finn (1990) distinguishes between constructive and destructive multicultural education. In the latter category, he includes curricula that is, "designed to tell a particular group about themselves, their ancestors, their unique qualities, how superior they are, and how oppressed they have been (Finn 1990, p. A40).

In contrast, constructive multiculturalism "draws on the ideas, customs, and historical contributions from all our variegated groups into a unified curriculum that everyone studies" (Finn 1990, p. A40). A potential danger in this artificial dichotomy is that topics that are legitimate, but may not particularly contribute to the unifying theme, are dismissed as destructive multicultural education. Issues such as institutional racism and linguistic or gender discrimination are the types of topics that are legitimate areas of study, but prime candidates for dismissal as destructive multiculturalism.

Diane Ravitch (1990) distinguishes between the cultural-pluralist and the particularistic approach to multicultural education. The former "accepts diversity as fact, and the latter

195

seeks to attach students to their ancestral homelands as a source of personal identity and authentic culture" (Ravitch 1990, p. A44). It is certainly possible for students to become so engrossed in their ancestral culture that they develop ethnocentrism. However, it is equally possible for students to take identification with a narrow definition of nationalism to similar extremes. The development of a positive identification with an ancestral culture does not constitute a negative consequence of a multicultural curriculum. James Banks (1988) suggests that persons must develop positive ethnic identifications before they can develop a clarified national identification.

The curriculum should present the essential elements of the American Creed (dignity, individual freedom, equality of opportunity) as well as instances when society has veered from those lofty values. Efforts at defining appropriate multicultural content only as topics that contribute to a unifying theme are inherently suspect. They are attempts to filter multicultural content through a neoconservative prism and, in effect, define those ethnic perspectives deemed legitimate. This insistence on a unifying theme, where it may or may not be present, adds an artificial criterion in teaching that is likely to interfere with critical thinking and analysis. The goal of education should be to expose students to a wide range of information and allow them to draw their own conclusions. Attempts to limit the perspectives students learn, however well intended, will detract from this goal.

Another caveat about the potential politicizing tendencies of multicultural education is the possibility that some educators will define multicultural perspectives as "special interests." These educators generally view themselves as defenders of traditional and wholesome tendencies in curriculum and attempt to diminish efforts toward multicultural curricular reform with the special-interest label.

RESTRUCTURING THE CANON

Taking a new look at the canon of knowledge and how it

is presented in our public schools is an area that is certain to generate some controversy. An appropriate multicultural curriculum goes far beyond sprinkling traditional subjects with selected heroes, heroines, and accomplishments of persons of color. A restructured canon of knowledge will sometimes challenge the imagined worlds that many students inhabit.

Many traditional concepts taught in American schools will have to be re-examined or qualified. When we teach that Christopher Columbus discovered America, we need to qualify that the term "discovery" applies to making the existence of the Americas public to Europeans. Otherwise, teachers risk leaving the impression that places don't exist until Europeans see them.

The qualification or redefinition of a number of traditional concepts is likely to spawn some opposition from fellow educators who often contend that this task is too complex. Another contention is that revising the curriculum to reflect multicultural themes and perspectives is a laudable goal but cannot be undertaken because there isn't enough time to teach current content. This view assumes that all current material enjoys priority status and multicultural perspectives represent curricular frills. An appropriate question to those who contend this is: "Does the existing curriculum give an appropriate representation of the diversity found in American society?" If not, it is an appropriate task for teachers and administrators to re-examine the *status quo*.

Many teachers will feel highly constrained by the existing curricular guidelines in their subjects. These guidelines may be viewed as limiting what could or should be taught in a subject, rather than as minimum for course content. Curriculum guidelines must be viewed as malleable. Teachers have always interpreted the emphasis given to various topics and the manner in which curricular guidelines are met. Also, educators should be willing to serve on groups that periodically revise guidelines to insure they are reflective of nonsexist and multicultural perspectives.

197

As a rule, attitudes within and outside of education are more receptive to presenting multicultural perspectives in the elective rather than the core curriculum. The latter, by definition, carries the highest academic value and is the most resistant to alteration.

MULTICULTURAL EDUCATION REPRESENTS AN ACADEMIC QUOTA SYSTEM

Some resistance will emanate from those that claim multicultural education seeks to elevate to curricular status the perspectives of women, ethnic groups, and persons of color that could not have passed traditional and rigorous standards for curricular inclusion. In effect, these critics argue that multicultural-curricular reform represents an attempt to force diverse perspectives in areas of instruction where they are not really warranted (Krauthammer 1990).

Topics such as the writing of the United States Constitution must reflect that this document was written by a white, elite, male segment of the American population at that time. However, it is entirely appropriate to raise questions in teaching this subject such as: "Why were there founding fathers and no founding mothers?" "How were the interests of persons not present during the writing of the constitution treated by that document?" It is important to discuss these types of issues, or we risk leaving the impression that the only types of people at the time capable of constructing such a document were those who received an invitation to the Philadelphia convention.

POTENTIAL FOR COMMUNITY RESISTANCE

There are two, often diametrically opposed, views of the role of public schools. One suggests that the experiences students have in school should be a direct reflection of that community's views and values. The other view holds that schools should provide students with a window to the world and teach information and perspectives that may not be widely discussed in the community. Depending on the nature of the community, these two views are not necessarily conflicting.

The goal of reflecting diversity in the curriculum can meet community or parental resistance. This is particularly true if it results in students learning material that was not part of their parents' academic experience. In one south Florida school district, plans were implemented to fully integrate African American content throughout the American history curriculum. In most settings, the plan went well, but resistance was particularly strong in high schools with the highest average-median income. Well-educated parents lodged complaints such as: "Why does my son/daughter need to learn this information when I don't know this and I am a successful person?" Another objection was: "How is this material going to relate to higher S.A.T. scores or help students find better jobs?"

This example helps illustrate that resistance can emanate from any point along the income or education continuum. Educators must communicate to their constituents that multicultural perspectives provide more varied and accurate conceptions of an academic discipline. These perspectives are valuable for all students but are particularly needed by students living in small, homogeneous communities.

Educators must not be dissuaded from multicultural curricular reform by the possibility of resistance. However, there are some points to keep in mind in this effort:

- Know your community and try to forecast and address possible objections in advance.

- Ensure that new information or perspectives being incorporated fit well within the academic discipline.

- When adding new course information that is not treated in the textbook, document it well.

- Enlist in advance the support of departmental colleagues, school administration, and district curriculum-specialists to the highest degree possible.
- Correlate new information to the maturational level of students.

POTENTIAL FOR RESISTANCE FROM COLLEAGUES

Many colleagues view curriculum as a dynamic entity in the educational process and will provide valuable assistance in assessing their disciplines from multicultural perspectives. Others, however, may see a multicultural focus in the curriculum as an added burden to be shouldered. Lack of familiarity with new content and cultural perspectives can promote feelings of obsolescence.

If multicultural curricular review is teacher-initiated, care must be taken to share new materials and expertise with colleagues who don't have that familiarity. When school districts initiate curricular review, it should be followed by workshops, courses, or other opportunities for faculty to become conversant with new materials and issues. Resistance to new approaches often melts when educators are comfortable with new academic content.

Colleagues may also be reluctant to become involved in multicultural curricular review if they think that this activity may label them as reformers. Teachers' behavior is molded, to a degree, by the school and district administration in which they work. Not all teachers regard curricular reform with the same zeal, but there are always less prominent roles that these colleagues may feel comfortable taking.

A final caveat regarding resistance from colleagues is that multicultural education goes beyond curricular review. It gives legitimacy to considering students' cultures and life experiences in the educational process. A few educators take the position that they teach "subjects" and not "students." They contend that academic content doesn't change depending on the background of the class. These educators are confusing product with process.

Multicultural education does not advocate changing exit criteria or competencies based on the cultural composition of the class. It does suggest, however, that teachers should be familiar with the research on the relationship of gender and cultural background to the learning process and adapt their teaching strategies where necessary (Cazden and Mehan 1989). The affective filter through which students learn is of major importance, and research on the significance of classroom atmosphere needs to be part of every teacher's preparation.

Current research on classroom interaction between teachers and students strongly suggests that female students and students of color do not receive proportional attention from their teachers (AAUW, NEA; 1992). These practices are often unintentional. However, all students need to be treated with similar dignity and attention in practice as well as in theory.

CONCLUSION

For multicultural education to move beyond its current embryonic stage in American education, it is imperative that its advocates understand the strength it brings to the curriculum as well as the pitfalls to its implementation. Critics of multicultural education have argued that open and legitimate discussion of cultural differences in schools will promote ethnic balkanization. Supporters of multicultural education have generally felt that the failure to recognize the pluralistic nature of this nation and world in the curriculum has contributed little to building a national consensus (Viadero 1990). It also has not added to students' abilities in critical thinking.

With regard to multicultural perspectives, too many of our students inhabit "imagined worlds." These imagined worlds are composed of persons largely like themselves and are places where knowledge of other cultural traditions is limited and

201

diversity is seen with skepticism. World views are rooted almost exclusively in their national identity.

Too many of our students do not understand that the information they possess may be incomplete or that it doesn't allow them to think critically. These shortcomings are not confined to any particular region of the nation or to the public sector of education. The relative dearth of knowledge about the non-European roots of American society can be found in students of differing ability and achievement levels.

Perspectives on the role of women and racial and ethnic minority groups remain largely the province of academic specialists. Shifting information about these groups from the periphery to the core of the curriculum is part of the goal of multicultural education.

Currently, multicultural education is seen by some as an effort primarily benefiting students of color. It must be seen as an attempt to broaden the perspectives of all students, particularly those who are members of the majority group. This latter conception, although more difficult to implement, has a much broader intellectual base.

American educators also need to reflect on the notion that there are attitudinal derivatives of knowledge, or lack of knowledge. Students rightfully posit their trust in schools to distill a highly complex body of knowledge and to teach them a representative sample of the whole. If there are entire areas, traditions, or groups absent from what schools choose to impart, it is not an illogical conclusion for students to think that there was not much of substance in those areas. It follows that students' academic experiences can support misperceptions or even prejudice by default, if not by design.

Multicultural education aims to reduce the gap between the academic distillation of the human experience and the world students perceive. In short, multicultural education is a curricular vehicle through which formerly inaudible voices can be heard.

REFERENCES

American Association of University Women; National Education Association (NEA). 1992. *How schools shortchange women.* Washington, DC: NEA.

Banks, J. A. 1988. *Multiethnic education: Theory and practice.* Boston: Allyn and Bacon.

Cazden, C.B.; Mehan, H. 1989. Principles from sociology and anthropology: Context, code, classroom, and culture. In *Knowledge base for the beginning teacher,* edited by M. Reynolds, 47–57. New York: Pergamon Press and American Association of Colleges for Teacher Education.

Finn, C.E. 1990. Why can't colleges convey our diverse culture's unifying themes? *The Chronicle of Higher Education* 13 June 1990, A40.

Krauthammer, C. 1990. Education: Doing bad and feeling good. *Time* 5 February 1990, 78.

Ravitch, D. 1990. Multiculturalism, yes; particularism, no. *The Chronicle of Higher Education* 24 October 1990, A44.

Viadero, D. 1990. Battle over multicultural education rises in intensity. *Education Week* X (13): 1.

AFTERWORD

THE LEADERSHIP CHALLENGE IN MULTICULTURAL EDUCATION

by Cherry A. McGee Banks

We have an opportunity to improve education in the United States by increasing student achievement, reducing prejudice, and helping students to develop the skills and knowledge needed to build a more just and democratic society. The authors in this volume described the role multicultural education can play in restructuring schools to attain those goals. Each author addressed a specific component of multicultural education and provided a clear rationale for why schools must change. Examples of how schools can change were included throughout the volume.

James A. Banks' chapter is an excellent departure point for exploring the specific components of multicultural education discussed by the other authors in this volume. He defined multicultural education as a process, an idea, and a way of teaching. He noted that multicultural education is an interdisciplinary field. Its key concepts are taken from several disciplines, including sociology, political science, anthropology, and history. The integrative and interdisciplinary nature of multicultural education requires that teachers not limit multicultural content and perspectives to a single unit or subject. Teachers should integrate multicultural content and perspectives throughout their curriculum and teaching. In fact, multicultural content and insights should permeate the entire social system of the school because specific norms, values, and goals are implicit throughout the school's environment, including its instructional materials, policies, counseling program, and staff attitudes as well as its hidden and formalized curricula.

Many educators are committed to increasing their effectiveness in multicultural classrooms and believe that they have a responsibility to reflect cultural diversity in their teaching. As Geneva Gay stated in her chapter, teachers often say, "Tell us what to do and we will do it." She urged educators to recognize that multicultural education is a sophisticated, complicated, and demanding endeavor that cannot be implemented easily or quickly, but requires serious professional preparation. Gay believes teachers must be empowered to make their own high-quality multicultural decisions. She terms that process *contextual decision-making* and provided readers with an excellent foundation for examining the process of making decisions, assessing the adequacy of the decisions, and placing multicultural interventions into the proper scope, sequence, and context of other classroom operations.

Implementing the kinds of structural changes that Banks discussed and developing the range of skills described by Gay requires leadership. James Kouzes and Barry Posner (1987), two researchers in the field of leadership, have identified five practices that are common to individuals who have been able to successfully implement important changes in their institutions. The practices are: challenging the process, inspiring a shared vision, enabling others to act, modeling the way, and encouraging the heart. These practices can be used by teachers and administrators who want to accept what Kouzes and Posner term the *leadership challenge* and to implement an effective multicultural program in their classrooms and schools.

CHALLENGING THE PROCESS

According to Kouzes and Posner (1987), challenging the process involves searching for opportunities, experimenting, and taking risks. Teachers challenge the process when they look for opportunities to improve their teaching and are willing to take the risk to implement new methods, content, and perspectives into their curriculum. Multicultural education, therefore, provides a means for teachers to challenge the educational process. Educators can use the information presented in this volume as a foundation for examining their current way of teaching and learning more about multicultural education.

Carlos Díaz's discussion on the changing nature of the U.S. population identified one of the key factors motivating educators to learn more about multicultural education and challenging their current way of teaching. People of color are increasingly becoming a more visible proportion of the American mosaic. According to the American Council on Education (1988), at least half of the students who attend public school in 25 of the nation's largest schools are students of color. By 2020, students of color will constitute almost 40 percent of the school-age population. And demographers project that by the year 2000, approximately one-third of the U.S. population will be people of color.

Norene Daly and Deborah O'Dowd pointed out that the educational process will not only be challenged at the K-12 level; it will also be challenged at the university level. Implementing changes in curricula, textbooks, and teaching practices at the K-12 level will require teachers who have the skills, attitudes, and knowledge to put those changes into effect. Teachers will need an educational background that will enable them to work with a diverse student population and to help all students become effective citizens in an interconnected global society. To prepare teachers to address the changing nature of the K-12 student population, schools of education now and even more so in the twenty-first century will need to include multicultural education in their certification and graduate programs.

INSPIRING A SHARED VISION

To be effective, leaders must inspire a shared vision. According to Kouzes and Posner (1987), a shared vision is a positive, hopeful dream of the future that embodies the mutual interests and concerns of others. Leaders use their genuineness and communication skills to inspire others to make a commitment to the vision and work toward achieving a common purpose. By creating a sense of urgency and excitement around the vision, leaders are able to inspire others to act. In 1965, Martin Luther King, Jr. (King 1965), addressed civil rights marchers in the Selma-to-Montgomery march. He said: "Let us move on in these powerful days, these days of challenge, to make America what it ought to be. We have an opportunity to make a better nation." King's words challenged the people of this nation and inspired a generation to make the ideals of justice and equality real for all Americans.

Multicultural education is an idea that can inspire a new vision for American education. The authors in this volume described the role multicultural education can play in addressing the educational challenges of the United States. Those challenges include restructuring schools so that students from all ethnic, racial, social-class, language, and special-population groups have an equal opportunity for academic success. Teachers who are multicultural leaders can use the multicultural vision to inspire the students in their classrooms to reach extraordinary levels of achievement.

However, teachers cannot order their students to be committed to a multicultural vision; they must inspire their students to make a commitment to it. Teachers who are multicultural leaders must identify the hopes and dreams of their students and help them see the exciting possibilities that their futures hold. They inspire a shared vision by showing their students how they will be served by a common purpose. Teachers must understand their students' needs and have their interests at heart. Only through an intimate understanding of their students' hopes, dreams, aspirations, and values can teachers enlist their students' support and create a shared vision.

Too often, major elements of schools, such as testing and evaluation, alienate students and parents because they do not embody their hopes, dreams, aspirations, and values. In this volume, Ronald Samuda and John Lewis discussed the issue of evaluation in multicultural classrooms and concluded that many of the traditional protocols for assessing students are not effective for students of color. An evaluation system that is fair, designed to identify student potential, and serves as a vehicle to support student development can help inspire a common vision for students and teachers who are multicultural leaders. Samuda and Lewis recommended the "L.P.A.D. and the K-ABC as more appropriate assessment devices for testing minority children."

Creating a school environment where language diversity is respected can also assist teachers in inspiring a shared vision. Communication is a key factor in this quest. Communication webs involving teachers and students, parents and teachers, and students and students are essential for communicating a shared vision. Sonia Nieto observed that in an environment where monolingualism is perceived as an asset, many of the languages that students bring to school are not given the visibility and respect that they deserve. In a shrinking world, the perception that monolingualism is an asset must change. To be effective in the twenty-first century, U. S. citizens will need to communicate with larger numbers of people who do not speak English as their first language. Nieto argued that all students should have access to bilingual and multicultural programs.

ENABLING OTHERS TO ACT

Enabling others to act involves fostering collaboration and empowering others. Trust, teamwork, and collaboration are essential attributes of this process (Kouzes and Posner 1987). Teachers who are multicultural leaders recognize that they cannot achieve success by themselves. They must enlist the support and assistance of others to implement the multicultural vision in their classrooms and schools. The team should include teachers, administrators, students, and parents (Comer 1980). Communication among them can help team members gain a sense of ownership for decisions that are made. When people feel empowered and have a sense of ownership, they are more likely to use their energies to produce the desired results.

Karen Swisher's chapter on learning styles illustrated how teachers can use information about their students' cultural values and behaviors to design effective teaching strategies. When teachers implement more effective teaching strategies in their classrooms, they empower their students and create an environment where parents are more inclined to collaborate with the school. Therefore, implementing more effective teaching strategies enables both parents and students to act.

Swisher provided her readers with a sophisticated understanding of learning styles. She explored both the promises as well as the limitations of the learning-styles paradigm. While information on learning styles holds great promise for more effective instruction, Swisher cautioned the reader to be aware of the tremendous potential for using a student's learning style as a justification for discrimination or as an excuse for failure. Teachers must always be sensitive to the difference between group norms and individual differences. The awareness of the characteristics of groups does not necessarily result in information that teachers can use to understand individual learners.

Enabling others to act is not limited to traditional students. Teachers who are multicultural leaders must be prepared to work with a diverse student population that includes special-education students. They can enable special-education students to act by addressing assessment bias, bias in placement decisions, identification of and service to language minority students, and other issues identified in this book by Christine Sleeter and Constanz Hartney. Sleeter and Hartney also pointed out that students of color and students from low-income families continue to be placed disproportionately in special education, and are underidentified for programs for gifted students. The authors noted that special education is not unique in this respect; it reflects the overall bias found in schools.

Enabling students to act also requires that teachers address issues related to gender. Jane Bernard-Powers showed

209

that gender continues to be an important influence on the educational experiences and achievement of male and female students by examining the role of gender bias in SAT tests, classroom organization and instruction, and five curriculum areas: social studies, reading, math, science, and computer education.

MODELING THE WAY

Visions cannot become realities without a plan. Kouzes and Posner (1987) state that modeling the way involves setting an example, planning small wins, and focusing on key priorities. Multicultural leaders must set goals with clearly identified milestones. They must also distinguish their values and their beliefs. If their behavior is inconsistent with their stated beliefs, parents, students, and colleagues may lose respect for their ideas.

Teachers who are multicultural leaders become role models for their colleagues, students, and members of the community. Serving as a role model requires maintaining congruency between values and actions. Teachers who are multicultural leaders cannot say one thing at staff meetings and something else in the teachers' lounge. Multicultural leaders must be consistent, persistent, and always vigilant (Kouzes and Posner 1987).

Prejudice remains a problem in U. S. society, and it is a serious barrier for multicultural leaders who are trying to model the way. Prejudice and discrimination are problems that will not be eliminated until schools implement an active and thoughtful campaign against them.

In this volume, Glenn Pate suggested that schools begin by establishing and publicizing their policies of antidiscrimination and antiprejudice. He recommended that teachers use checklists such as those developed by James Lynch (1987) to examine their practices and the results of their efforts. Pate said that in order to be effective, teachers must develop a sophisticated understanding of both their students' cultures and the tremendous diversity within ethnic and cultural groups.

Modeling the way is not limited to teachers. Students must also model the way for each other and for members of their communities. The competencies that Ricardo Garcia discussed can serve as the foundation for helping students gain the skills to function effectively with diverse peoples, cultures, and people who speak different languages. The human rights approach Garcia recommended encourages students to take responsibility for their own learning and enter a social contract in which everyone has rights and the responsibility to respect the rights of others. It also requires teachers to make their classrooms a community of scholars who are in pursuit of learning. When disputes occur, Garcia recommended that teachers guide students through negotiations that help them develop skills in conflict resolution so that they will not feel that they are forced to resort to violence. If students can learn to resolve differences peacefully in their classrooms, they will have the moral competence to resolve differences peacefully within the broader human community.

ENCOURAGING THE HEART

Implementing change is difficult. Teachers who are involved in multicultural change must engage in new behaviors and have new expectations for themselves and their students. The process of becoming a multicultural leader can be exhausting and frustrating. Teachers can very easily become disenchanted and tempted to give up and return to their old ways of teaching. By following Sleeter and Hartney's recommendation to work collectively for change, educators can support each other. They can recognize the accomplishments of their colleagues, celebrate their achievements, and provide emotional support to their colleagues so that they will be encouraged to continue their efforts. Sleeter and Hartney noted that when educators work together, they can be a powerful voice for change. They suggested that educators learn to manage personal and professional stress by using techniques such as relaxation training, self-talk, thought stopping, and environmental planning.

Teachers must also encourage the hearts of their students. Students come to school because they want to be winners, not because they want to be labeled as losers. Teachers who are multicultural leaders show students from diverse ethnic, racial, gender, social class, and special population groups how they can be winners. Teachers can show their students that they genuinely care about them as people by giving individual awards, holding group celebrations, sending thank-you notes to parents when they help their children with homework assignments or help with other activities, and demonstrating that they care in other ways that reflect the cultures and values of their students.

Valerie Ooka Pang's discussion of change at the Martin Luther King, Jr., Elementary School in New Haven, Connecticut, illustrated how school climate can encourage the hearts of students, parents, and teachers. She reviewed seven characteristics identified in effective school research: school-community dialogue, high expectations, teacher involvement in decision making, the principal as instructional leader, focus on developmental and social skills, and regular student monitoring.

CONCLUSION

To be effective in the twenty-first century, education must embrace the multicultural vision. The multicultural vision can serve as a foundation for addressing the challenges and reaping the benefits of increasing levels of diversity in the United States population and increasing requirements for American participation in a global society.

Transformational leadership is needed to implement the multicultural vision. Transformational leaders are intricately connected to their followers through shared values and goals. They work together and are motivated by the same vision (Burns 1978, pp. 141–254). Multicultural leaders are needed at all levels. Teachers who are multicultural leaders challenge the process, inspire a shared vision, enable others to act, model the way, and encourage the heart. They embrace the multicultural vision and use that vision to guide change and to accomplish extraordinary things in their classrooms.

REFERENCES

American Council on Education. 1988. *One-third of a nation.* Washington, DC: American Council on Education.

Burns, J. Mac Gregor. 1978. *Leadership.* New York: Harper and Row.

Comer, James P. 1980. *School power: Implications of an intervention project.* New York: Free Press.

King, M.L., Jr. 1965. Address to marchers. Selma, Ala.

Kouzes, James M.; Posner, Barry Z. 1987. *The leadership challenge.* San Francisco: Jossey-Bass.

Lynch, James. 1987. *Prejudice reduction and the schools.* London: Cassell.

ANNOTATED BIBLIOGRAPHY

by Cherry A. McGee Banks

Banks, James A. 1991. *Teaching Strategies for Ethnic Studies*. 5th ed. Boston: Allyn and Bacon.

This is an excellent source book for teachers who want to integrate ethnic content into the curriculum. Key concepts, goals, current trends, and a rationale for ethnic content in the curriculum is included in the first part of the book. The second part includes historical overviews, teaching strategies, and teaching materials on African Americans, Asian Americans, European Americans, Mexican Americans, and Native Americans.

Banks, James A. 1988. *Multiethnic Education: Theory and Practice*. 2nd ed. Boston: Allyn and Bacon.

Theoretical, conceptual, philosophical, and definitional issues related to multiethnic education are explored in this book. It is an important resource for teachers who seek a strong foundation in multiethnic education.

Banks, James A.; McGee Banks, Cherry A., eds. 1989. *Multicultural Education: Issues and Perspectives*. Boston: Allyn and Bacon.

This book is designed to provide teachers with the skills and knowledge they need to work more effectively with male and female students from various ethnic, cultural, social, and religious groups. Contributors from several disciplines help present a wide range of perspectives.

Derman-Sparks, Louise; A.B.C. Task Force. 1989. *Anti-bias Curriculum: Tools for Empowering Young Children*. Washington, DC: National Association for the Education of Young Children.

This publication shows how teachers can help young children recognize and confront gender, racial, and other biases against people who are different from themselves.

Gay, Geneva; Baber, Willie L. 1987. *Expressively Black: The Cultural Basis of Ethnic Identity.* New York: Praeger.

This is a collection of 14 essays that explore kinship, family ties, leadership, communication, and other cultural characteristics of African Americans.

Hampton, Henry; Fayer, Steve. 1990. *Voices of Freedom: An Oral History of the Civil Rights Movement From the 1950s Through the 1980s.* New York: Bantam.

This companion to the PBS television series *Eyes on the Prize* presents the voices of women, children, and men who participated in the civil rights movement.

Heid, Camilla A., ed. 1988. *Multicultural Education: Knowledge and Perceptions.* Bloomington: Indiana University.

Research and practice are blended together in this book, which includes chapters on preparing future teachers and teacher perceptions of race, class, and gender.

Hilliard, Asa G.,III; Payton-Stewart, Lucretia; Obadele Williams, Larry. 1989. *Infusion of African and African American Content in the School Curriculum: Proceedings of the First National Conference.* Morristown, N.J.: Aaron Press.

The authors provide information on the roles Africans and African Americans have played in world history. Most of this information is not found in general textbooks. Chapters by Ivan van Sertima and John Henrik Clarke provide information on curriculum development.

Jones, Jacqueline. 1985. *Labor of Love, Labor of Sorrow: Black Women, Work, and the Family From Slavery to the Present.* New York: Basic Books.

This is an engrossing, vivid, and comprehensive account of the work and family life of African American women.

King, Edith W. 1990. *Teaching Ethnic and Gender Awareness: Methods and Materials for the Elementary School,* 2nd. ed. Dubuque, Iowa: Kendall, Hunt.

Multicultural and global education are brought together in this book, which includes both a rationale for addressing diversity and activities that teachers can use with elementary school students.

Lynch, James. 1987. *Prejudice Reduction and the Schools.* London: Cassell.

This is an important resource for teachers; it includes activities, resource lists, bibliographies, and a theoretical framework for understanding the nature of prejudice and for developing the skills to combat it.

Meier, Kenneth J.; Stewart, Joseph, Jr.; England, Robert E. 1989. *Race, Class, and Education: The Politics of Second-Generation Discrimination.* Madison: University of Wisconsin Press.

School districts with at least 15,000 students and with one-percent African American enrollment were included in this revealing study of discrimination in education.

Ramsey, Patricia G. 1987. *Teaching and Learning in a Diverse World: Multicultural Education for Young Children.* New York: Teachers College Press.

This book includes practical and theoretical information on multicultural education that can empower teachers with the knowledge and skills they need to tailor multicultural goals and activities to the specific needs of their students.

Schniedewind, Nancy; Davidson, Ellen. 1983. *Open Minds to Equality: A Sourcebook of Learning Activities to Promote Race, Sex, Class, and Age Equity.* Englewood Cliffs, N.J.: Prentice-Hall.

Multicultural role plays, case studies, dilemma stories, and other activities for reading, math, science, and social studies are included in this book.

Sleeter, Christine E. 1991. *Empowerment Through Multicultural Education.* New York: State University of New York.

Ways in which multicultural education can be used as a

vehicle to empower teachers, students, and members of oppressed groups are identified and discussed by authors.

Sleeter, Christine E.; Grant, Carl A. 1988. *Making Choices for Multicultural Education: Five Approaches to Race, Class, and Gender.* Columbus, Ohio: Merrill.

This book is an overview of five theoretical and philosophical frameworks, that educators can use to address race, class, gender, and disability in teaching.

Sleeter, Christine E.; Grant, Carl A. 1988. *Turning on Learning: Five Approaches for Multicultural Teaching Plans for Race, Class, Gender, and Disability.* Columbus, Ohio: Merrill.

This book includes 48 lesson plans based on the theoretical framework presented in its companion volume described above. The lesson plans are organized into the five approaches that Grant and Sleeter have identified.

Vold, Edwina Battle, ed. 1992. *Multicultural Education in Early Childhood Classrooms.* Washington, DC: National Education Association.

This book gives specific techniques for broadening the multicultural dimensions of every subject area in early childhood education.

THE CONTRIBUTORS

Cherry A. McGee Banks is Assistant Professor of Education at the University of Washington, Bothell, and the founder of the Educational Materials & Services Center (EMSC). EMSC is an educational initiative that focuses on improving education for special population groups, such as ethnic minorities, women, and exceptional students. Dr. Banks is also editor and publisher of *Multicultural Leader*, a quarterly newsletter, as well as co-author of *March Toward Freedom: A History of Black Americans*, co-editor and contributing author of *Multicultural Education: Issues and Perspectives*, and contributing author of *Education in the 80s: Multiethnic Education*.

James A. Banks, Professor of Education at the University of Washington, Seattle, has written numerous books on multicultural education and on social studies education. These include *Teaching Strategies for Ethnic Studies*, 5th edition; *Multicultural Education: Issues and Perspectives* (with Cherry A. McGee Banks); *Multiethnic Education: Theory and Practice*, 2nd Edition; and *Teaching Strategies for the Social Studies*, 4th Edition. In 1986, Dr. Banks was named a Distinguished Scholar/Researcher on Minority Education by the American Educational Research Association. He is a past president of the National Council for the Social Studies.

Jane Bernard-Powers is Assistant Professor of Elementary Education at San Francisco State University, California. She is currently serving as Associate Editor of *Theory and Research in Social Education*, and on the executive board of the College and University Faculty Assembly, an affiliate of the National Council for the Social Studies (NCSS). Dr. Bernard-Powers is a past chair of the Advisory Committee on Gender and Social Justice for the NCSS. Her publications include *Gender and the Social Studies Framework*, *The Girl Question in Education*, and "Sex Equity in the Social Studies" with Carole Hahn in *The Handbook for Achieving Sex Equity in Education*.

Norene F. Daly is Professor and Dean of the College of Education at Iowa State University, Ames. She began her career as an elementary and secondary school teacher and has been an elementary school principal, district-wide reading coordinator, and federal projects coordinator. She is a past president of the American Association of Colleges for Teacher Education, past chair of the Executive Board of the National Council for Accreditation of Teacher Education, and past president of the Association of Independent Liberal Arts Colleges for Teacher Education. She also served as Chair of the Executive Committee of the U.S.A.-China Teacher Education Consortium. Her publications have been in the areas of multicultural education, reading education, adult education, and teacher education.

Carlos F. Díaz is Assistant Professor of Multicultural Education in the College of Education at Florida Atlantic University, Boca Raton. He was a contributor to the document *Curriculum Guidelines for Multiethnic Education*, issued by the National Council for the Social Studies, and a contributing author to *Teaching Strategies for Ethnic Studies*. He has served as a reviewer for the Ethnic Heritage program of the Department of Health, Education, and Welfare and as a consultant to state and local school agencies.

Ricardo L. Garcia is Professor of Education and Director of the Division of Teacher Education at University of Idaho, Moscow. His research areas encompass bilingualism, second language development, and sociocultural factors in teaching and learning. His ongoing research projects include a study of the language preferences of Cuban Americans and a study of the religious literacy of teacher-education students. His textbook, *Teaching in a Pluralistic Society*, was reissued in 1991.

Geneva Gay is Professor of Education at the Center for Multicultural Education at the University of Washington, Seattle. In addition to teaching courses on multicultural education, she has written more than 80 articles and book chapters, and she consults nationally and internationally on issues related to curriculum development, instructional strategies, and staff development for multicultural education. She is the co-editor of the recent publication, *Expressively Black: The Cultural Basis of Ethnic Identity.*

Constanz Hartney is Assistant Professor in the School of Education, University of Wisconsin, Parkside, where he teaches educational psychology and exceptional education. Dr. Hartney completed a psychology clinical internship at Curative Rehabilitation Center, Milwaukee, where he specialized in spinal cord injury treatment, headache management, and stress management. He has had extensive clinical experience as a psychologist in private practice, treating individuals for chronic headache and chronic stress. His patient load still consists of many teachers (especially special-education teachers) with whom he conducts stress management.

John Lewis is Assistant Professor in Educational Psychology and Counseling at McGill University, Canada. He has written several papers and chapters in the area of intercultural counseling.

Sonia Nieto is Associate Professor and Director of the Cultural Diversity and Curriculum Reform Program at the School of Education, University of Massachusetts, Amherst. Her research focuses on multicultural education and curriculum, with a particular interest in parent involvement in education, the image of Puerto Ricans in children's literature, and the role of bilingual concerns within multicultural education. Dr. Nieto's many publications include her most recent book *Affirming Diversity: The Sociopolitical Context of Multicultural Education.*

Deborah J. O'Dowd is a former instructor of multicultural, nonsexist education at the College of Education at Iowa State

University, Ames. Before that appointment, she was employed in the Title VII Program of the Davis School District in Davis, California, where she provided primary language instruction in academic subjects to students with limited-English proficiency.

Valerie Ooka Pang is Assistant Professor at San Diego State University, California, where she teaches multicultural education and educational foundations. Her articles have appeared in *Harvard Educational Review*, *Social Education*, and *Educational Forum*. She has also contributed to *Empowerment Through Multicultural Education*, edited by Christine Sleeter. Dr. Pang's research focuses on curriculum and instruction, mental health of Asian American students, and teacher/student interactions.

Glenn Pate is Associate Professor at the University of Arizona, Tucson, where he teaches undergraduate and graduate courses in equity and prejudice. Having been raised in a segregated community, he has had a long-standing interest in prejudice. He is also active in studying and teaching about the Holocaust so that the lessons learned from it can be applied to the future. He has conducted a definitive study of how textbooks in the United States treat the Holocaust.

Ronald J. Samuda is a visiting Professor and Consultant at Nova University and Adjunct Professor of the Universities of British Columbia and Simon Fraser in Canada. Dr. Samuda has taught at San Francisco State University, California, and at Richmond College of the City University of New York. He has served as Director for the Assessment of Minorities at Educational Testing Service, Princeton, New Jersey, and as Assistant Dean and Director of the Center for Ethnic Studies at Columbia University Teacher's College, New York. In 1975, he was appointed professor and chairman of Counseling at Queen's University and Professor Emeritus in 1988.

Christine E. Sleeter is Associate Professor of Education at the University of Wisconsin, Parkside. Her articles appear in journals, such as *Journal of Education, Harvard Educational Review, Teachers College Record,* and *Review of Educational Research.* Her books include *After the School Bell Rings, Making Choices for Multicultural Education, Turning on Learning* (all three co-authored with Carl Grant) and *Empowerment Through Multicultural Education.*

Karen Swisher is Assistant Professor in Curriculum and Instruction and Director of the Center for Indian Education at Arizona State University, Tempe. She is an enrolled member of the Standing Rock Sioux Tribe of North Dakota. In her current position, she is responsible for teaching a section of a required multicultural education course in addition to directing the research and service activities of the Center for Indian Education. Trained as an elementary teacher and administrator, she has had experience in public schools and in a school operated by the Bureau of Indian Affairs.